Chasing the and following the Roe

by

Ian Alcock

Illustrated by Diana E. Brown

Published by Sauchenyard Press
PO Box 3
Aboyne
Aberdeenshire
AB34 5YB

Copyright © 1998 by I. C. N. Alcock (text) and Diana E. Brown (drawings)

First published in the UK in 1998

ISBN 0 9534447 0 8

All rights reserved. No part of this book may be reproduced or transmitted in any form or by any means, electronic or mechanical including photocopying, recording or by any information storage and retrieval system, without permission from the Publisher in writing.

Printed by
Meigle Printers Ltd.
Galashiels
Selkirkshire
TD7 4BD

Contents

Introduction		i
A Brief History of Deer Forests and the Scottish Highlands	Page	1
Management of Red Deer	Page	10
Clothing for the Hill	Page	15
Equipment for the Hill	Page	17
Rifle and Practice	Page	20
Taking the Shot at a Deer	Page	27
Red Deer Stalking	Page	34
The Hill	Page	44
Culmination of the Stalk	Page	50
Venison in the Larder	Page	54
Red Deer Hinds	Page	58
Breeding of Red Deer	Page	65
Hind Range	Page	71
Judging Age	Page	76
The Development of Woodland Stalking	Page	82
Roe Deer	Page	84
Stalking Roe	Page	91
The Roe Deer Rut	Page	101
Paint, Pins and Teeth	Page	107
Roe Does	Page	114
Home Smoking	Page	123
Rifle for Deer and Shooting Seasons for Deer	Page	127
Lyme Disease	Page	129
Index	Page	130

Introduction

Thirty years ago if one mentioned deerstalking to most people the term would inevitably refer in their minds to stalking red deer on the open hills in the Highlands. Woodland stalking was then really only the pursuit of a few enthusiasts. Since then deerstalking has undergone substantial change, primarily due to its commercialisation. Woodland stalking is now a pastime enthusiastically pursued by thousands of people from all walks of life, and moreover provides necessary control over the rapidly expanding populations of woodland deer, which have spread remarkably throughout Britain in the past quarter of a century.

To some extent red deer stalking in the Scottish Highlands has been commercialised since the beginning of the nineteenth century, which is to say for two hundred years. The history of deerstalking in the Scottish hills seems not to be well known to most people, especially to some of those who clamour that red deer have destroyed the natural habitat and prevented the regeneration of native trees, or those who claim that deer forest owners have selfishly exploited their hunting grounds by expelling people to make way for deer. Those who have taken the trouble to study the history of Scotland will appreciate that the idea that deerstalking is a comparatively modern pastime, introduced by wealthy industrialists from the south who bought Highland estates in late Victorian times as holiday playgrounds, is a fanciful myth. As, indeed, also is the notion that a couple of hundred years ago Scotland was clothed in woodland, much of it indigenous Scots pine.

A Brief History of Deer Forests and the Scottish Highlands

It is important to appreciate that the ancient term 'forest' did not have the same interpretation in the past as it generally does now. It did not necessarily mean large areas of woodland, neither was a forester in ancient times a person involved in the tending of trees. The word forest derived from the Latin word *foris*, meaning out of doors, or *forestis* meaning the land that was outside the enclosed area or *parcus*, the park. The forester was more akin to what these days would be called the gamekeeper. References to a dictionary will show that forest can still mean a large tract of uncultivated land, which may or may not be wooded. Early hunting forests were Dartmoor and Exmoor, and of course The New Forest, which was created by William I, the Conqueror, as one of his personal hunting territories.

The early Kings of Scotland were just as addicted to hunting as those in England, although their forest laws were never so severe as those south of the Border. Even in the thirteenth century the royal hunting preserves were numerous and covered many areas of Scotland, up the east coast as far as Inverness, and in some parts of central Scotland, and even right up as far as Ross-shire.

Study of old manuscripts shows that from the thirteenth to fifteenth centuries the Forest laws were just as concerned with trees as they were with hunting. Even then trees were seen as valuable, both for timber and for fuel. These Forest laws made continual reference to grazing, indicating that there were open spaces, to pannage (the right to allow pigs to feed there), and vert, which was the right to cut wood.

It has to be remembered that throughout history the population has grown steadily, which has meant an ever increasing requirement for food and shelter for people. This meant in turn the necessity of clearing land for growing crops or for improving grazing for livestock, and the cutting of timber for use in building houses. In those early centuries many of the prime movers of agricultural development and economic progress were the monasteries and abbeys, and large parts of Scotland were controlled by the clergy, sometimes by gift of the king, and at other later times apparently in dispute with him. The large ecclesiastical buildings, to say nothing of the growing towns and villages, all used vast quantities of timber for buildings and furniture, and wood for implements and fuel. The value of the timber was recognised amongst other ways in the fact that if someone forfeited their land for some reason, often they were allowed to take with them the timber from the buildings. Centuries later, during the Highland Clearances in the north of Scotland, those evicted from their dwellings also carried with them the timber from the buildings when they could.

In the old deeds it is recorded that in 1250 the monks of Kelso were allowed to take timber from the land to repair buildings only if they gave the woods some 20 to 30 years to recover from the cutting, and the construction of sheep shelters were supervised to prevent waste. Even in those days sheep were numerous, with records showing over 6,000 of them, belonging to James I, grazing in Ettrick Forest.

In pre-historic times it is reckoned that the valleys and sheltered lower slopes of the hills in Scotland were wooded, with dense scrub in some of the uplands, as well as swamps and moors. In the lowlands oakwoods grew on the heavier soils, and these gave way to pine, ash and birch at higher altitudes. In the Highlands birch was the most common wood and native evergreens were a little more widespread than oak, but, according to V.G. Childe in *Prehistory of Scotland* (1935) dense forest did not occur on the high ground and woodland was patchy and scattered. Much of the land now classified as deer forest never was thickly wooded in historical times, and the idea that a large part of the Highlands was clothed in swathes of Caledonian Forest, consisting of Scots pine, even during the past seven hundred years, is largely myth.

As well as deforestation by the monasteries and abbeys to convert land for agricultural use, timber was required in ever increasing quantity for building, as well as for industries such as charcoal burning, iron smelting and shipbuilding, and in parts of lowland Scotland salt making used significant amounts of wood. By the thirteenth century a timber trade had developed and timber was imported from Scandinavia and Prussia. In 1457 the Scots parliament advocated that landlords incorporated in their leases provision for the planting of trees and the making of live hedges of wood and broom. In 1504 this parliament showed much concern that the wood of Scotland was 'uterlie distroyit' and tried to encourage lairds to plant small areas of woodland where such was not present. James IV imported wood for ships' masts from the Baltic and from France, and by the beginning of the sixteenth century a significant timber trade had developed between the north, from Inverness, to southeast Scotland. Timber from Rothiemurchus was shipped down to Edinburgh.

It is difficult to judge how local or severe was the wood shortage, and whether this was principally around the areas of population and economic growth, but it is clear that generally there was a shortage of timber of the quality required for building ships and large buildings. Nevertheless the Scottish Forest laws guarded the wood as closely as the grazing and game. In the thirteenth century a man could be fined eight cows for the first three wood cutting offences, and fined £10 on a fourth conviction. The cutting of trees, especially oak and maple, meant prosecution in court. By the year 1500 the apparent shortage of timber resulted in fines being increased to £5 for the theft or destruction of wood anywhere in the country, and in 1535 the death penalty was even introduced for a third woodcutting offence in forests. Tenants were often allowed wood for building purposes, but by the fifteenth century parliamentary legislation controlled wood, and enclosures of woodland began to appear to protect this, and not merely for the sake of the game that it might contain.

Thus it can be seen that as far back as five hundred years ago there was already a shortage of trees and woods in Scotland. So far as natural regeneration of the native trees is concerned, one has only to study old farm leases going back this far to appreciate that the shieling system was an important part of Scottish life, and a study of old maps, or of the ground itself, where ruins or larochs abound in almost all the glens, will reveal the high populations of hill country in the past. How people survived in those places is a matter of wonder to those with the benefits of the comforts of modern society, and it is difficult to conceive the subsistence living of these remote communities. Nevertheless, such research reveals that the places where deer now feed were occupied in the past by humans and their livestock. The shieling system was universal, and old farm leases show the right of the tenants to graze their livestock, cattle, sheep and goats, in the forest areas. Many of the remote hills and glens offered valuable grazing to domestic livestock in summer, and it was the custom for these to be driven up into the hills, often from long distances, to take advantage of this grazing. This transhumance involved whole families moving up into the hills to live during the summer where the menfolk or boys could tend their flocks, whilst the women made butter and cheese from the milking and spun cloth from the wool.

Probably the shieling system would have afforded encouragement to the regeneration of those woods that were left, especially when the livestock involved were mainly cattle, rather than sheep and goats. The cattle would have trampled and dunged the ground, creating seed beds for the seedlings, but concentrating on the hill grasses for feeding. However, during the eighteenth century several dramatic changes took place in the Highlands particularly after the terrible retributions and changes following the battle at Culloden in 1745, which led to the break-up of the existing clan systems and the obligations of their menfolk to fight when required. Gradually the drift from the land began, the situation of the clan chiefs and lairds changed, and the sheep came to the hills in great quantities.

At the beginning of the eighteenth century the lairds, or clan chiefs, owned great tracts of land in the Highlands; but these were of little value and produced meagre revenue. Much of England's wealth had been derived from sheep, hence the significance of the Woolsack on which sits the Lord Chancellor in the House of Lords. In around 1760 flockmasters began to appreciate the opportunities of grazing sheep in the hills; in particular wethers (castrated male sheep, kept for three or four years for their larger wool fleeces and then sold as mutton), which could be grazed profitably upon higher ground that might not be suitable for breeding ewes. This prospect of increased income from their land appealed to the lairds, and the sheep flocks belonging to new large scale tenants began to appear on the hills. By 1785 these sheep had found their way as far north as Ross-shire, and by 1820 they grazed the hills throughout the Highlands in their hundreds of thousands, as far north as the north of Sutherland. In some areas, particularly these northern counties, the existing crofting tenants who contributed little to the lairds by way of rent, were evicted to make way for the sheep and many were given new accommodation on the coast. These were the areas where the infamous Highland Clearances took place. The sheep and their shepherds were responsible for further reduction of tree cover.

During these times little interest was taken in deer stalking except for the provision of venison for the laird's own consumption. At the beginning of the nineteenth century there were probably only half a dozen forests with large numbers of deer, though even on these the shieling system still took place, and the best grazing on the hills was traditionally given over for the use of domestic livestock during the summer months with the annual transhumance. Gradually deerstalking began to assume greater importance, as a possible source of income to the landowners. This was due partly to the appearance of daily coaches travelling north to Edinburgh from England, which allowed the keenest hunters to travel to Scotland, even though facilities for accommodation remained primitive, often necessitating lodging with the shepherds or other local inhabitants, there being then no shooting lodges available. In 1840 the introduction of the railway enormously eased the travel procedure and accelerated the interest in sport in Scotland.

Meanwhile the prosperity of the wool trade faltered in 1828, though recovered again, and by 1840 Scotland was producing in the region of a quarter of the country's wool. Sheep numbers in Britain had risen from a reported figure of 12 million at the end of the seventeenth century to over 35 million in 1868. Seven million of these sheep grazed in Scotland. Those blaming deer for the lack of woodland regeneration over this period should bear these figures in mind. Flockmaster tenants paid good rents for their grazing leases, and sheep took precedence over deer or grouse, and only a few forests reserved their ground for deer stalking. Although grouse and sheep could go together, and lairds could benefit from letting out some grouse shooting as well as from the grazing rent, deer competed with sheep for the grazing and were less popular.

However in 1860 a major change started to take place in this situation. Throughout the 1860's imports of wool from Australia rose steadily from 147 million pounds in 1861 to 259 million by 1870. Within a couple of years the wool price collapsed again, but this time continued its decline. At the same time mutton for consumption by the rapidly expanding industrialised urban population was being imported from Australia, New Zealand and Argentina. This heralded the end of the sheep boom. The flockmasters abandoned their leases, which they found had become profitable no longer, and the lairds found that a prime source of their income evaporated. Moreover, under the terms of the leases, many landowners had to take over the hefted sheep flocks, and found themselves having to sell off these abandoned and unprofitable flocks at less than the valuation costs. With little alternative use for the land they had no option but to give over the land to deer, and the number of deer forests increased. By 1883 there were 99 deer forests recorded, and by 1912 the number had risen to 202.

The number of grouse moors, which previously had also held sheep, declined. A report in 1871 quoted detailed figures for the estate of Invercauld, at Braemar in Aberdeenshire, which demonstrated that a deer forest could achieve an equivalent rent of 1s.1d. per acre, compared to 10d. only that could be derived from sheep, or an increase of 30%. However the proliferation of deer ground led to a saturation of the market, with supply exceeding demand. On the other hand the value of scarcer grouse ground rose.

The publication of the celebrated books by William Scrope and Charles St. John helped to fire the imagination of sportsmen in the south for deerstalking in the Highlands of Scotland, and the enthusiasm for the sport shown by the Prince Consort and the purchase of the Balmoral estate by Queen Victoria gave social impetus to Highland estates and their sporting opportunities.

William Scrope first rented Bruar on the Duke of Atholl's estate in Perthshire in 1822, having been given a reference by Sir Walter Scott. This beat of the estate covered some 135,000 acres, of which 30,000 were primarily grouse ground, 55,000 deer forest, and a further 50,000 with both deer and grouse. Scrope rented Bruar for ten years. In 1824 Edwin Landseer, then already a celebrated painter of animals, came to Atholl to study the area of Glen Tilt. He also was a friend of Sir Walter Scott, and possibly as a result of an introduction from him went to stay with Scrope at Bruar. As a result of his introduction to deerstalking there he became very keen on the sport and repeated his visit to Bruar in 1825 and 1826. This ultimately led to that most famous of British deer paintings, The Monarch of the Glen. This painting was originally purchased in 1851 by Lord Londesborough for 350 guineas. Later it fetched £6510 at auction in 1884. It was bought by Agnew's and sold in 1892 to Mr Barrett of Pear's Soap for the sum of £8000, a huge amount in those days. It was resold once again in 1916, during the First War, and bought by Sir Thomas Dewar for £5000 for his whisky company.

William Scrope's book The Art of Deerstalking was published in 1838, and his friends Edwin and Charles Landseer helped to illustrate this. Scrope had been a minor painter of landscapes for years, and it was probably his interest in the scenery and the hills that first took him to

Scotland. For the illustrations in his book he painted the backgrounds of the pictures and the Landseers painted in the animals and figures.

In those early days of deer forests the accommodation was rather primitive. Realising that in order to derive income from letting the stalking of the deer or the grouse shooting they had to provide accommodation for the tenants, some of the lairds erected shooting lodges or adapted existing houses for the purpose. The lodge at Bruar, when Scrope first rented it, did not meet his requirements, and at his request the estate altered and improved the building, whilst Scrope attended to some of the decoration.

With the coming of the improved travel arrangements, the trains from London to the north, the opportunities for sport in the Highlands became available more readily for other than hardy shooting enthusiasts prepared to rough it, and the prospect of wonderful family holidays in the invigorating Scottish air appealed to a number of rich industrialists and to professional men seeking relaxation from city life. Some of these rented estates and deer forests on long leases, some took them for the season, and others purchased the estates outright. In order to house their families and entourage of servants commodious lodges were built on many of these estates, and the whole tenor of the deerstalking scene changed to a rather grander affair. Red deer stalking became largely available either to those who could afford to lease a forest, or to those fortunate enough to know the owner of a Highland estate and be invited to be a guest.

A further development of importance took place that dramatically affected deerstalking, and this was the introduction of breech-loading rifles. These had the great advantage not only of easy loading but of certain firing in foul wet weather; and the overall accuracy of the modern rifles also improved, in the hands of the competent shots of course.

Around the middle of the present century the situation affecting red deer stalking in Scotland began to change again. As a result of higher taxation of income, inheritance tax, and general pressure of business, many of the families owning the Scottish estates could no longer afford the expense of running them, or could no longer afford the time for long holidays. Gradually either these were sold off, or the sport was once again rented out, usually by the week, and often with accommodation provided in the lodge, with the owners perhaps retaining only one or two weeks for themselves and their guests.

In more recent years the commercial letting of deer forests, and indeed of all shooting, has extended further, and these days although some forests still let their stalking by the week with an allocated number of stags, and of rifles to be allowed onto the hill at once, depending upon the number of beats and estate stalkers available, a large number of deer forests now charge by the stag and will contemplate letting stalking by the day. These changes have allowed access to red deer stalking to a much wider selection of sportsmen and sportswomen, and indeed of a variety of nationalities. Estates where the stalking is available only as the guest of the owner by his or her invitation are now very much the minority.

This change in the type of stalking availability has had inevitable influence upon the management of the deer herds and the attitude of the stalkers. At the same time the knowledge of red deer has increased dramatically in the past twenty years as a result of the introduction of red deer farming as an established commercial enterprise, which has meant that serious research into many aspects of the deer has been carried out in several parts of the world. A number of the old myths about deer and stalking have now been discredited.

Several authors of books on red deer stalking in the early part of the present century warned of the possible dangers of the commercialisation of the deerstalking. They pointed out that tenants leasing deer forests, particularly those doing so for perhaps only a season or for only a year or two, but sometimes also those on longer leases, had little incentive to take a long term view of the deer herd hefted to that area and inevitably would be more interested in their current sport during their tenancy. Thus there was the temptation to shoot the better beasts, and sometimes to shoot too many deer. Furthermore, tenants had no interest in improving the estates generally, planting trees, improving grazing for the deer and so on.

A further disadvantage was that the stalking tenants had interest only in shooting stags, the hind shooting being left to be carried out by the estate staff during the winter. With the short days in winter in the north, and the difficult weather conditions in the hills, culling sufficient hinds often became a problem. Hind stalking was rarely let out, and still is available only on a few forests, because estate staff under great pressure to achieve cull numbers find that having to take out a paying guest hinders the cull, since the guest is rarely sufficiently active to enable advantage to be taken of opportunities that may arise as well as the professional stalkers used to daily walking and stalking in the hills.

Even at the turn of the last century writers were voicing concerns about the deterioration in the quality of stag antlers and body weights. In 1905 one author wrote that the average quality of the deer had declined, and that neither the heads nor the weights were as good as twenty years previously. Some stalkers suggested that overstocking caused the decline and others pointed out that the deer were not so good as when the ground was first cleared of sheep. This complaint about the quality of the deer is still often voiced. However, just how accurate is such a claim is less easy to establish in practice. Examination of old estate records does not suggest that average weights have declined, if one allows for the fact that on the majority of forests traditionally only older stags of a certain size were shot for preference, especially where these were recorded and the records liable to be published at some stage. Estates took pride in showing high average weights. Examination of collections of antlers may be more informative, if these collections are comprehensive rather than selective. A good example is the collection, reputed to consist of 3000 antlers, which decorates the famous ballroom of the Mar Lodge estate in upper Aberdeenshire Deeside. Study of these suggests that in fact there has been little change over the past century in the mean antler quality of average hill stags, and the majority of those in the collection are unremarkable. The few exceptions, of fine heads, clearly derived from park stags that lived in the estate policies.

In some ways it is surprising that there has not been a noticeable deterioration in the quality of the hill red deer, since in many of the forests some of the best grazing and sheltering areas have been planted with trees, or reclaimed for agricultural use, thus denying the deer the best feeding and vital winter shelter.

Management of Red Deer

In the past quarter of a century a number of Scottish deer forests have changed considerably, with new owners who often have had no previous experience of owning Scottish deer ground, with several large estates split into smaller ones, and particularly with the increasing financial pressures that caused these estates to become more commercially minded in an effort to try to defray the ever increasing cost of running them, where mostly the prospect of operating at a profit is remote and the best that can be hoped for is minimizing the ongoing loss. Even where a deer forest may achieve profitable operation, in terms of return on capital the profit is likely to be derisory compared to alternative investment.

Two factors are pre-eminent in influencing the management of the deer. The first of these is tradition, and the second is the physical capability of shooting deer numbers. The type of terrain and habitat is all important in determining the type of forest and its deer holding capacity. Food supply, shelter, lack of disturbance, and height of ground, are all of importance in relative attraction to the deer. Some ground is primarily hind ground; other areas are favoured by stags. Hinds tend to favour lower ground with good summer feeding, where they can have their calves in security. Female deer, as with the females of other species – of which sheep are an obvious example – tend to become hefted to the place where they are born, and return to the same area in due course for their own calving. Experiments with recording red deer tagged as calves show that whereas most hinds live much of their time within a mile or two of where they were born, circumstances being equable, stags wander, and often travel significant distances, especially at the time of the rut.

For the recreational sportsman who has hired a week's stalking, or the chance of shooting a stag, on a deer forest, the question of the management of the deer may be of no direct concern, and the decision what to shoot and when to shoot, will be that of the professional stalker who takes him or her out onto the hill. The tyro must understand that whatever the circumstances, the estate stalker is in complete charge. This is one reason why the stalker usually carries the guest's rifle, apart from his probably being far fitter on the hill and therefore finding the burden less onerous. The stalker is thus in a position to hand the guest or client the rifle when, and only when, he deems it appropriate.

Because most deer forest owners are absent much of the year, and the letting of the stalking may be in the hands of agents, the responsibility of the resident professional stalker is increased, and very often the management of the deer is dependent upon him and his ideas. A few younger stalkers are becoming employed on deer forests now, replacing retiring men, and some of these have acquainted themselves with current information about deer and become familiar with modern knowledge. However, tradition still governs the approach to the management of the deer, and many estate stalkers and deer forest owners and those who advise them seem unaware of the continually increasing knowledge resulting from the research that has gone into red deer entirely as a result of the proliferation of deer farming in the past twenty years, not only in this country but in many parts of the world.

One of the great problems with the management of a deer forest, though, is that whatever management ideas the owner or stalker may have, putting these into practice is usually a matter of considerable difficulty by reason of the constraints of the seasons and the weather and the manpower available. The numbers of stags and hinds shot each season, particularly the former, are largely influenced by tradition. This in turn was probably influenced by the numbers that it was possible to shoot during the available season. For many estates the stag season, though theoretically commencing in July in Scotland, in practice is rarely a feasible proposition until late September, which means that it lasts only five or six weeks at the most. In July and August the stags are still putting on condition, or recovering from the previous winter and spring when feeding was poor, and their antlers are still growing then.

Without doubt, by the end of August and the beginning of September, when velvet has been shed and the stags are in hard antler, but not yet started to rut, they are in the finest condition. In previous centuries, when deer were hunted for venison as much as for sport, and the meat was of great importance, this was the season known as 'the time of grease', the period when the stags were at their fattest.

Not only is September the time of optimum weights for most stags, which can lose up to a third of their bodyweight during the rut, including all of their fat, but, because of this and the venison being recognised as being in the best condition then, venison prices are often at their highest at this period, dropping later as the rut proceeds and quality reduces and numbers of deer shot increase. There are several factors which tend to preclude stalking being concentrated upon this early part of the season. Firstly, most paying clients or guests are interested in obtaining trophy antlers, and so although most stags will be in hard horn by then, until the rut starts and the bigger or older stags start to look for hinds, many of these will not be seen. Secondly, those estates with grouse will be concentrating upon these until late September rather than upon the deer. Thirdly, until the first frosts and the change to cooler autumn weather Culicoides impunctatus, that terror of the Highlands, to both man and deer, the Highland Midge, renders much of the hill country unbearable. The stags remain for the most part on high ground, where cooling breezes can keep the midges and flies from tormenting them on their growing antlers, and they are not encouraged to leave the sanctuary of these draftier places even when first in hard horn until the first frosts kill the midges, or the rise in their testosterone levels provokes the overpowering urge to go to seek hinds in season.

In the last century, and especially in the centuries previous to that, the quality of venison was the most important factor in the pursuit of deer. Indeed, even earlier in the nineteenth century many or most deer forests ceased to stalk stags by October 10th or earlier, deeming the venison unfit for consumption with the rutting of the stags commencing. Nowadays the quality of venison seems to be regarded as a low priority with most deer forests and stalkers, since the emphasis is on the value of the stag as a trophy or as the object of a stalk, and in the case of hinds the emphasis is on numbers and the achievement of cull targets.

The latter, the achievement of culling the planned number of hinds, is often a daunting task for the estate stalkers, since, although the

Scottish hind season is from October 21st, the end of the stag season, until February 15th, and four months may seem a long period, in practice the weather reduces the opportunities substantially. If the weather is mild early in the winter the hinds tend to be found far out on the hill, which means that a great deal of time is involved in getting out to stalk them and then to bring the carcasses back to the larder, whilst if the weather is hard, bringing the beasts lower down and nearer to the lodge, snow and ice make the whole operation markedly more difficult. Moreover there are many days throughout winter when stalking hinds is rendered impossible by weather conditions.

It is often suggested that more opportunity should be made of letting out hind stalking to enthusiast clients or that the estates should utilise the willing assistance of fit and hardy amateur stalkers, but in practice this is often not a viable proposition. One cannot have too many parties out stalking on the hill simultaneously, since these disturb the ground for each other. A significant part of the skill in hill stalking results from experience of the particular hill ground itself, knowing the approach most likely to be successful in differing wind and weather, and also knowing the possible routes for extracting carcasses from the hill. Stalkers unfamiliar with the ground cannot contribute in this respect, whilst those casual amateurs, however keen, who are less fit than the professional stalker only tend to slow down the exercise. When it comes to deciding which hinds to cull, clearly, if the objective is to try to shoot several from a group, or at least take both a hind and her calf, it is quicker if the stalker does not have to explain the required beasts to a guest rifle, but can make his own decision and shoot accordingly.

The decisions upon the numbers of both stags and hinds to be shot each season on a deer forest, and upon what type of beasts of each sex should be shot, these days are open to a degree of controversy, particularly since most of these decisions have been based upon tradition. However, these traditional figures have often been based upon the totals achievable from the forest in a normal season and not merely upon a planned cull figure judged in the context of the assumed deer population of the area of ground covered. In many cases these total target culls for both stags and hinds may still be appropriate. The increase in the total red deer population of Scotland claimed to have taken place over the past few decades, albeit stabilised for the past ten years, has not been experienced in all areas, but has been more localised and arisen often by the establishment of the deer in new ground. The requisite management of the deer on an individual forest depends upon many factors relating to deer numbers, habitat, deer impact upon land bordering the estate, and the objective of the policy decided upon.

Clothing for the Hill

The traditional clothing worn on the hill by professional stalkers, of tweed plus fours and deerstalker hat, has evolved from experience and with good reason. The tweed deerstalker hat, with ear flaps that can be tied under the chin, may appear strange to people unfamiliar with hill conditions, but the sense becomes apparent with experience of usual stalking weather. There are occasions when the ear flaps are welcome to protect from icy blasts, and the tapes tied under the chin enable the headgear to be kept in place in the strong winds often experienced on the high tops of the hills, whilst the fore and aft peaks shelter the face and back of the neck from rain, especially when lying watching deer. Some fore and aft hats are made with the peaks too hard; these are not satisfactory, because, when lying in a position to shoot, the back peak can push on the collar of a jacket and tilt the fore peak irritatingly too far forward over the face.

Woollen tweed is ideal wear for the hill, since it is insulating and warm, yet allows air to pass through it. Tweed also has excellent waterproof quality and will keep out wet conditions longer than many other materials, and, more importantly the wool cloth, like woollen stockings, retains the insulation and warmth even when wet. Both dry easily too. It is because woollen tweed has been found to be the most satisfactory material in these respects, coupled with its camouflaging properties, and lack of shine when wet, unlike most man made materials, that it has become so universally popular for wearing in Scottish hill conditions, not merely with stalkers. The garments described as plus fours these days are really more correctly what should be described as plus twos. Proper plus fours are noticeably baggier, coming lower down the leg, and in fact are actually more practical for hill walking, since the extra overhang of the tweed gives greater leg movement, and easier bending of the knee when climbing steep ground. These days popular garments with many low ground shooters are described as breeks, and are effectively a type of breeches. They are even more economical in material than plus twos, and as a result permit much less comfortable knee bending, and will be found to be much less suitable for hill work than the traditional garments.

Recommended footwear for the hill consists of strong leather boots with well treaded rubber soles. Tackety, or nailed, soles on boots are fine on some ground, but where rock is encountered these are both slippery and noisy and should be avoided. A strong waterproof outer garment is also recommended in wet weather. Many stalkers wear waxed cotton jackets or coats made from man made material alleging complete waterproofing yet ability to 'breathe' and let out condensation. The problem with most of such garments is that they become shiny to some degree when wet, and very obvious on the hill. Wool clothing avoids this.

Equipment for the Hill

Most experienced hill stalkers prefer not to venture out onto hill ground without a good strong stick. Tyros who go out without a stick will soon discover why this is regarded as an essential piece of equipment for walking on rough or wet ground, and especially where both are encountered, as on most deer forests. A good strong comfortable stick is a great aid to walking, often acting as a third, stabilising, leg. It has other uses too, such as acting as a steadying prop when spying with telescope or binoculars , as a useful handle to which to attach a rope if dragging a beast becomes necessary, and, not least, for sticking into the ground as a marker for where one may leave the rifle cover, piece bag, telescope, or other impedimenta, when proceeding on a final crawl to get into position for a shot. The inexperienced stalker will be astonished at how easy it is, in the excitement of the final approach, to forget precisely where these were left, for hill ground looks surprisingly different and confusing when viewed from different angles, and equipment lying in the grass or heather can be elusive to spot. The ideal stick for stalking on the hill is not the long shafted crummock (from the Gaelic cromag, meaning a crook or hook) beloved by folk for walking round Game Fairs, which are fine for ordinary strolling, but rather a stout walking stick, possibly slightly longer than one normally used for walking on low ground. It needs to be stout and not fancy, since it is not uncommon for the user to slip and risk breaking the shaft.

A telescope is useful on the hill for long distance spotting, but is not necessary, particularly if one is being taken out by a professional stalker, who is likely to carry one. Telescopes are not always easy to use on the hill, where light conditions may be poor, and the casual stalker is probably better advised to carry a good pair of binoculars instead. In wet weather, all these instruments tend to get the glass misted, or even water inside the lenses when used in heavy rain. A good tip is to carry a number of absorbent paper kitchen towels or sheets of soft toilet paper in an inside pocket, which can be used for drying the lenses of binoculars or telescopes or rifle sights, and may have other uses too. The wearing of a waistcoat underneath jacket or sweater has the advantage of providing several handy inside pockets for such items that may be required for emergency use. A couple of spare bullets wrapped in such paper is another wise precaution in case others get lost somehow during crawling, or whatever. A particularly useful spare, which is small enough to be accommodated in a waistcoat pocket, is a monocular. This can be very handy if conditions are consistently wet to the extent of finding binoculars difficult to see through because of continuous rain. It can be extremely frustrating should this occur during a final approach when careful spotting may be vital. A dry monocular can sometimes be invaluable under such circumstances.

There are undoubtedly differing views on telescopes and binoculars for use on the hill. Traditional three-draw telescopes have become collectors items these days, since possibly only one firm still supplies new ones, and these are expensive: but second hand stalking telescopes with leather shoulder cases can occasionally be found in sale rooms and bought at auction. They are useful for the long distance spotting and examination of deer, but not really necessary for the casual stalker, for whom binoculars will suffice. There is no need for great magnifying power from binoculars, and bearing in mind that there are many days on the hill when light conditions are not the best, reasonable light gathering properties are often an advantage. Nevertheless, the most important factor is that these have to be carried, even when crawling, and so a convenient small size has advantage, especially if it is possible to tuck these easily inside a jacket or coat for protection. The ideal binoculars for woodland stalking, where large light gathering lenses are essential if used at dawn or dusk, are often quite unsuitable for conveniently taking on the hill.

A further essential piece of equipment is a good knife. This must be sharp and strong. There is no need for this to be large, and a blade three to four inches long is adequate. Many stalkers use folding knives, preferably with a locking blade, and these may be perfectly acceptable under most circumstances; but a rigid one piece knife, where the steel of the blade continues through the handle to give maximum strength, is far better, and avoids any risk of the knife accidentally shutting on one's hand if, for instance, it is necessary to 'stick' a beast that is not completely dead and motionless. There is no need at all to have a fancy hand made knife, beautiful as these may be, and excellent knives with hollow ground blades of good quality steel can be purchased for modest prices. A small knife can often be carried in its sheath in a pocket, obviating the slight risk of this being lost during crawling, when worn on a belt. The professional stalker taking out a client or guest rifle is sure to carry a knife, but nevertheless it is always a sensible insurance for the casual stalker to take his own as a precaution in case of one being lost, or to enable him to carry out the task of dealing with a beast himself.

For hill stalking a further vital piece of equipment is a rifle cover for carrying and protecting the rifle. An ordinary shotgun slip is no use because these are not wide enough to allow for telescopic sights. The rifle cover needs to be strong and waterproof, with a sling for carrying it. Good quality canvas is best. Covers made from plastic or some other man made materials are unsuitable because these are often shiny, especially when wet, which makes them visible at a long distance. The purpose of the cover is not only to protect the rifle and sights from inclement weather, but particularly to ensure that these remain clean and dry when crawling during a stalk; and carrying out such manoeuvres will be found to be very much easier and less fraught with problems when the weapon is adequately protected. The rifle only needs to be withdrawn from its cover and a round inserted into the chamber ready for firing when the time comes for a shot to be taken.

Rifle and Practice

The subjects of rifles, their calibres and types, the ammunition used, and the relative suitability for different types of stalking and ability to kill deer efficiently, are all ones about which a great deal has been written, and about which individual stalkers have widely differing views. With increasing restrictions upon firearms, ownership of different rifles for different purposes becomes more difficult, and those new to stalking may find it more convenient to opt for a single rifle that can be used for all British deer species. In which case a suitable calibre might be .243, which is neither excessively heavy for roe or muntjac yet is adequate for shooting rutting red deer stags on the open hill. Where large woodland red deer or rutting fallow bucks are possible quarry a heavier calibre may be preferable.

Some enthusiasts may be interested in loading their own ammunition and experimenting with a variety of bullet weights and powder loads, but those content to rely on factory produced ammunition, having experimented with different types, should decide upon the most suitable and stick to this, because, as they may discover during their trying with different bullets, some of these may shoot to a slightly different position from others in some rifles. In the case of .243, 100 or 105 grain bullets are fine for both red deer and roe, but 75 grain bullets are too light for satisfactory use on red deer, and in some rifles may shoot several inches differently from the heavier 100 grain. However the subject of calibres and ballistics is a separate one.

Given a rifle of suitable calibre, the important thing is not to argue about the relative merits of different calibres, and how much deader some render a beast than others, but to become entirely familiar and competent with one's own rifle. It is absurd to spend a lot of money on a rifle and a telescopic sight, and possibly spend a lot more money on some deerstalking, and then to quibble over the cost of ammunition used in order to sight in the rifle properly. One should practice with the rifle at length until achieving confidence in one's ability with the weapon.

A recent trend has been the use of bipods attached to the rifle to allow steady aim. Whilst these have some merit to allow accurate shooting, they must never be allowed to be regarded as a substitute for acquiring competence and confidence in shooting the rifle without such an aid. When one is taught to shoot with a rifle the lesson should be instilled that one must never rest the barrel or fore-stock of the rifle on a hard surface for shooting. This is because the firing of the rifle and the passage of the bullet will cause an upward flip of the barrel as a result of the lack of give in the surface below the rifle. Thus if the rifle is being rested on a rock to give steady support, for instance, either the shooter's hand should be underneath supporting the rifle, between this and the rock, or the barrel should be supported on something soft like a rolled up gun cover or a haversack or somesuch. Consequently, reliance upon shooting with a bipod has two considerable disadvantages. The first of these is that if the shot has to be taken from a position where the bipod cannot be used, or particularly if it is necessary to take a quick shot in another direction or at a running wounded animal, the user may not be sufficiently accustomed to shooting without such an aid. The second problem is that the bipod may well result in a change in point of bullet impact from that of use without it.

A test was carried out in 1995 with 23 different rifles, with and without fixed bipods. This found that the difference of mean point of impact between use with and without a bipod was 2.2 inches at 100 yards, with a variation between 1 inch and an alarming 7 inches. This suggested that either one should never shoot without a bipod on that particular weapon, or one should never shoot with one, but that certainly the user must be aware of the potential difference in point of impact, depending upon the particular rifle. This may mean that if the rifle sighting is significantly altered by shooting with such a rest, then should a situation arise where a shot without its use is necessary the user may have to aim off appropriately to allow for this, which is a highly unsatisfactory situation in, say, the case of a hurried shot at a wounded animal. The problem does not appear to occur when a bipod is used on a rifle with fully-bedded fore-stock barrel sections, and the deviations were said to arise where the barrel is free floated, especially in relatively light, slim, typically sporting type rifle stocks. Some bipod manufacturers claim that no change in point of impact occurs whether the bipod is used or not used, but the important point is that the user of the rifle with a bipod should test the effect on his particular weapon so as to be aware of the situation.

An additional inherent hazard with the use of a bipod, as well as the possibility of encouraging longer shots to be taken, is that shooting from a low or prone position, where the bullet is going to travel parallel with the ground, increases considerably the danger in low ground or woodland, compared to taking a standing shot, where the angle is likely to be downward. Consequently the situations where a safe shot may be taken off a bipod in comparatively flat country must be limited.

Practice with rifle shooting is something with which the proficient deerstalker can never have enough. Many people will not have the facilities for frequent practice with their stalking rifle, being limited to shooting on ranges or perhaps on some safe ground nearby. However, practice need not be restricted only to use of the particular large calibre centrefire rifle. It may be that opportunities present themselves for target practice, or better still rabbit stalking, with a .22 rimfire, or failing that an air rifle. The latter makes little noise, has a limited range and therefore less danger, and ammunition is very cheap. Constant use of an air rifle is an excellent way of practicing rifle shooting; especially of learning to shoot confidently from different positions.

There is a substantial difference between shooting at paper targets and live quarry, however, and the objective of the deerstalker is to kill his quarry instantly, rather than to achieve tight groups on paper. Shooting at targets on a rifle range is vital practice for two purposes. To ensure that the rifle is correctly sighted in for the appropriate range and is capable of accurate and consistent shooting, and to test and improve the ability of the person using the rifle. Once these have been achieved satisfactorily, then the practice for deerstalking in reality should start. An admired South African big game hunter, who was regarded as a particularly fine rifle shot, once remarked that 'a tight group on a paper target is fine, but in the field the first shot must be final'. Writing in 1901 Wilmott Dixon pointed out that "Neither in sport nor war will any object remotely resembling the regulation target ever present itself to the sharpshooter. In war and sport a man has to find his target, to pick it out from surroundings calculated to render it indistinguishable." He went on to observe the importance of being able to assess range when shooting in the field, suggesting that in practical shooting tests the ranges should not be disclosed.

Horatio Ross, one of the outstanding shots of the past, writing in his Introduction to the Handbook of Deerstalking by Alexander Macrae published in 1880, also emphasised the importance of being able to judge distances on the hill and to practice at shots more in keeping with reality. "Every young stalker – and some old ones too – will derive advantages, even with modern express rifles, if, when they have an opportunity of practising on hilly ground, they devote some time to firing at stones, or any other mark, in every possible position. Try down and up hill, on level ground, and from the side of a steep hill to an opposite hill." He emphasised that he made it a rule never to fire at a deer beyond the range of 150 yards, and wrote the advice for stalkers "I beseech them to keep in mind, when getting near the end of their stalk, the words – one hundred and fifty yards". This is sound advice still today, even with modern high powered flat shooting rifles and telescopic sights.

The advice to try shooting up and down hill is apposite. This is because the angle of a shot can affect the point of impact of the bullet. This situation is unlikely to be encountered often by a woodland stalker, since even though in hilly ground the range is unlikely to be long enough to affect the shot when coupled with a steep angle; but it certainly does happen, and the stalker should take note of the effect of steep angles. When shooting steeply uphill, and downhill, the bullet is inclined to go high. It may surprise some people to realise that the bullet goes high both uphill and downhill and not the reverse in one direction.

The effect of angle is easily calculated. At an angle of 30° up or down the effect, for, say, a .243 rifle, is as if the zero range is 136 yards instead of 100 yards. With an angle of 45° the equivalent is as if sighted in at 180 yards instead of 100 yards, whilst at an angle of 60° it will be as if the zero range was 266 yards. This means that at a range of 100 yards and an angle of 60° the bullet will go unexpectedly high if the angle is ignored.

Various computer software programmes are available from which, by feeding in the information of the calibre, bullet weight, type of ammunition etc., one can calculate a chart or graph of the trajectory of a bullet over certain ranges. This information is handy to have, not only to enable the shooter to understand the ballistics and trajectory flight of a bullet at different ranges, but also it can save a deal of trouble and walking to check targets. For instance, a certain .243 sighted in for accuracy at 100 yards for 100 grain bullets and factory ammunition, will shoot $1/2$-inch high at 35 yards. If the bullet is dead centre on a target at 100 yards there should be a $1/2$-inch variation up at 35 yards and down at 135 yards from centre. This should be sufficient level of accuracy for stalking deer of any size. Knowing these figures the user need then only sight in the rifle to be $^{1}/_{2}$-inch high at 35 yards, with the knowledge that this will then be dead centre at 100 yards.

Although shooting at live targets at long ranges is to be discouraged, nevertheless part of the experience of becoming familiar with a rifle should include that of taking some long shots, say up to 300 yards, simply for the purpose of gaining the experience of how the rifle performs at such a range. In case of an emergency, perhaps a wounded beast running off, it is useful to know this so that one has a good chance of stopping the animal should the situation arise. Similarly it is a good idea to have tried a few shots at a moving target, if it is possible to arrange this. On the Continent, and indeed in many countries, shooting at moving deer or boar during driving manoeuvres is regarded as normal, and in some countries, such as Holland, there is an obligatory test involving shooting at a running boar target, which one is required to take and pass if one wishes to participate in driven boar shooting. Apart from a few culling operations, such as moving roe and fallow deer in woodland in winter to waiting rifles to achieve the required winter cull targets, driving deer does not take place normally in Britain these days. Nevertheless the situation can arise when a stalker is required to shoot a moving deer, to kill a wounded beast, or perhaps to kill an animal damaged as a result of a motor accident or some other injury. So, again, stalkers should have had the experience of shooting at a moving target with a rifle, even if this might never have to be put into practice with a live animal.

The majority of shots fired on the open hill are taken by the shooter lying prone. In woodland stalking very few shots can ever be taken in this position and most shots will be taken standing, perhaps supported by a tree or stick, from a high seat, or either from a sitting position or kneeling. The sitting position may sometimes be necessary on the hill too. Consequently practice with a rifle should include shooting from all these positions so that the shooter becomes accustomed to them. As already mentioned, much of this practice can be carried out conveniently in the back garden, or in a field, using an air rifle to completely familiarise oneself with these different positions and become quite used to shooting from them.

Many deer forests have a traditional rifle range near the lodge, with a life-sized iron deer as a target. Most professional stalkers, taking out a client or guest, ask that these take two or three shots at a target before going out, in order to check both the rifle sighting and the competence of the shooter. Most guests prefer to do this anyway. All stalkers, especially if they have travelled with the rifle, or are using a borrowed rifle, ought to fire three shots at a target before going stalking to ensure that the rifle is properly sighted and not been accidentally knocked. The advantage of an 'iron stag' (or roebuck) target is that it represents a far more realistic objective than a paper one. This is because it has no bull's-eye painted on it. A real deer has no spot marked on it at which to aim, so the shooter therefore has to decide upon the point at which he should shoot, and then hit this. Such a test reveals not only his or her skill with the rifle but also their knowledge about where to place the bullet for the required clean kill. It is no good being a superb shot with a rifle if one is unfamiliar with the anatomy of a live target and therefore the practical bull's-eye at which one should aim.

A recent report noted that some golfers had taken to practicing their strokes in the dark using fluorescent balls, claiming that this enabled them to concentrate upon their swing better. This is somewhat reminiscent of the Duke of Leeds, who took over the lease of Mar Lodge estate, in Aberdeenshire, about the middle of the nineteenth century. He was a strict disciplinarian and expected all sportsmen going to the hill to be of sufficient standard in shooting. His order was often one shot, one stag per day, and he was rightly very angry if a beast was wounded and not secured. He expected all his guests to be able to sight accurately and fire their rifles within three seconds. On stormy days, apparently, the Duke would assemble his guests in the gun room for rifle practice. In those days the rifles used percussion caps. When fired, these gave sufficient blast to extinguish a candle, if accurately fired, at two or three feet range. The guests were thus lined up in front of lighted candles, so that when the rifles were brought to their firing position on their shoulders the muzzles would be about a foot from the candle. Time keepers were appointed and a score given from one to five seconds taken to fire and to be accurate enough to extinguish the candle. The Duke regarded three seconds as the desirable maximum for mounting the rifle and firing. This training must have improved the skill of his guests considerably, for quick confident, almost instinctive, shooting is most likely to be successful, compared to the wavering indecision of those taking a long time over firing their shot. The emphasis was on practice to achieve confidence and competence.

Most stalkers require to travel to their stalking ground, and this invariably means putting the rifle in a vehicle, possibly with other gear, and perhaps with other people, or even a dog. During the process it is all too easy for a rifle sight to get knocked without this being realised. A useful piece of equipment that enables one to check against such a disaster without having to fire the rifle, and indeed most useful for approximately sighting in a new rifle to save using up a lot of ammunition in achieving hits on the target of reasonable accuracy, from which fine zeroing can commence, is an item called a collimator or a bore sighter. This small instrument, easily carried in a pocket if required, resembles a small telescopic sight. They are generally supplied with three arbors, or metal rods, with ends expandable by a screw. These arbors, of different sizes, by means of their adjustable ends, will fit a variety of barrel calibres from .22 to .45, and so will accommodate most sporting rifles. The arbor fits below the small sight and into the end of the barrel of the rifle, and the sight is lined up with the rifle's sights. The collimator sight has a grid resembling graph paper. When the rifle is correctly sighted in one checks where the rifle sights or telescope reticule appear on this grid and records the position. Thereafter one is able to check the rifle's telescopic sight and ascertain whether it has been knocked out of alignment by inserting the collimator and ensuring that the position of the reticule of the rifle's sight is the same on the collimator grid as previously recorded.

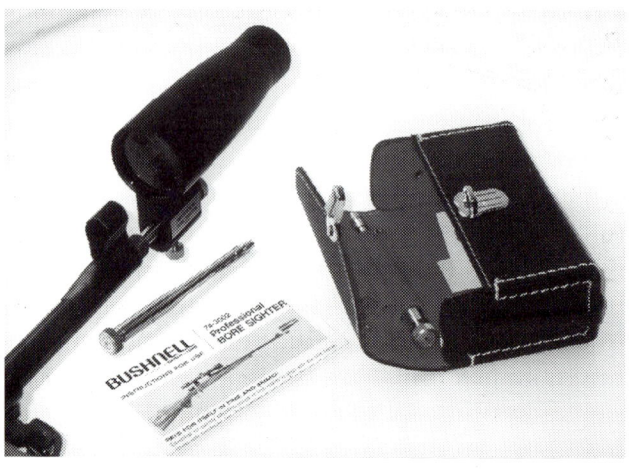

Taking the Shot at a Deer

The neophyte will discover that there is a considerable difference between shooting at a paper target on a rifle range or at some inanimate object and actually shooting to kill a deer. Apart from the obvious fact that no target is painted on the deer, more often than not the animal will not be standing in an ideal position for a shot, and, whether at the culmination of a long stalk on the open hill or a careful approach in woodland, there will be an element of excitement, and perhaps breathlessness too, with which to contend. Occasionally this feeling of excitement will turn into an altogether more alarming condition known to stalkers as 'buck fever'. This affliction strikes most stalkers at some time or another, and occurs occasionally, and usually inexplicably, with even seasoned professionals who shoot large numbers of deer regularly. It is not necessarily the reaction to aiming at a particularly fine stag or buck, nor when finally getting the chance of a shot at a long pursued animal. Neither does it seems to be sparked off simply by the fear of making a poor shot; though it may be something to do with the innate concern about the possibility of not killing the quarry cleanly. Buck fever manifests itself not merely in the nervous wobbling of the rifle sight, especially in unsteady or difficult conditions, but in a very much more exaggerated form that makes it impossible to take the shot properly. The stalker may find himself sweating profusely and shaking violently and completely unable to hold the rifle still. The golden rule must always be followed, that if a person using a rifle is unhappy about the shot and not confident, then the shot must not be taken. In the case of experiencing an attack of buck fever, or even of finding the sights wobbling too much, the shooter should put down the rifle and relax until composure is recovered, which is likely to be the case after just a couple of minutes. It is far better to have the self control to refuse to take a shot than to risk wounding a deer by taking a shot when in retrospect one might feel that one should not have done so at that moment.

Many stalkers are unaware of the true size of the various deer species, and thus of the target points on these animals. With full concentration upon a roe buck it may look quite a sizeable target at 80 yards, whilst a red deer stag can look positively enormous at that range, with his heart/lung area offering an apparently large easy target. Before considering shooting at a roe buck, for instance, it is as well to appreciate that a good animal may only be as high at the top of its shoulder as the level of the knee of a tallish man, being perhaps around 25 inches tall at the shoulder. Weighing 23-27 kgs liveweight an adult roe is not as heavy or as large as many large dogs, such as a German short-haired pointer or a vizsla. Roe bucks and does are much the same average size, whereas in the other species found in Britain the males tend to be noticeably larger and certainly heavier than the females. A mature red deer stag on open hill ground might weigh between 90-125 kgs liveweight, compared to 65-90 kgs for a hind, and woodland red deer may be considerably heavier. Nevertheless the shoulder of a hind only comes up to the waist of a man and that of a stag a little higher. If one observes deer and sheep

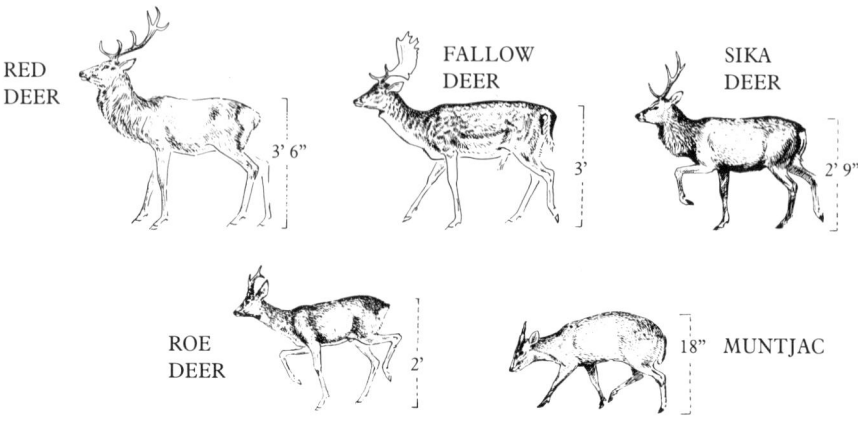

on the skyline one appreciates that the actual body size of a hill hind is much the same as that of a ewe, but the deer looks bigger because of her longer legs.

Thus, when it comes to shooting at a deer it is necessary to get the relative size in perspective. This assists in the all important factor of correctly judging the range of the target. It is surprising how sometimes seeing deer in the distance out in the open it can be deceptive at first glance deciding whether the animal is a roe deer or a red deer, or indeed a sika. Without initial perspective by which to judge size it can be difficult to be certain without other identification; and lacking the relative size differential guide the estimation of distance can be confusing. The easy means of identification is the colour of the animal's caudal patch, or backside, and the shape of this. The white or pale caudal patch of a red deer extends over its tail onto its back, whereas that of a roe does not. In some parts of England and some continental areas roe deer have no white or creamy coloured caudal patch round the tail in summer, but all roe have a bright white patch, capable of being flared when alarmed, in winter coat (except continental black roe). Sika also have a very bright white caudal disk, which is not only much whiter than that of a red deer, but lacks the light brown obvious tail in the middle of the buff or dirty white rump area of the red deer.

Whilst most knowledgeable stalkers agree that the sensible and desirable target area for a deer is that of the heart and lungs, some professionals, and other riflemen who fancy their skill, advocate neck shots as preferable, since this does not damage meat. The tyro should never attempt a neck shot at deer save in exceptional circumstances, and should never attempt a head shot. The latter can inflict the most appalling damage on an animal without killing it, and a deer running off with its jaw broken will die a horrible lingering death. There are two reasons why a neck shot should be avoided. The first is that whilst a successful one will drop a deer in its tracks, it will not necessarily kill the animal but only paralyse it from the neck down. The second is that the target area is a small one and working out precisely where the vertebrae of a stag run in a thickly maned neck is not easy. Failure to smash the vertebrae will not drop the animal, or may knock it down only for it to recover and run off. In any case, the humane killing of the animal is the priority and should be considered more important than the possibility of a little meat damage.

Without doubt, the best way to discover the lay-out and precise positioning of the organs and skeleton of a deer is to carry out the gralloching and butchering of carcasses, taking note of the anatomy in the process. By studying the bullet entry hole, the possible exit hole, and the internal damage caused, one learns by experience where the organs lie and the effect of a shot through these.

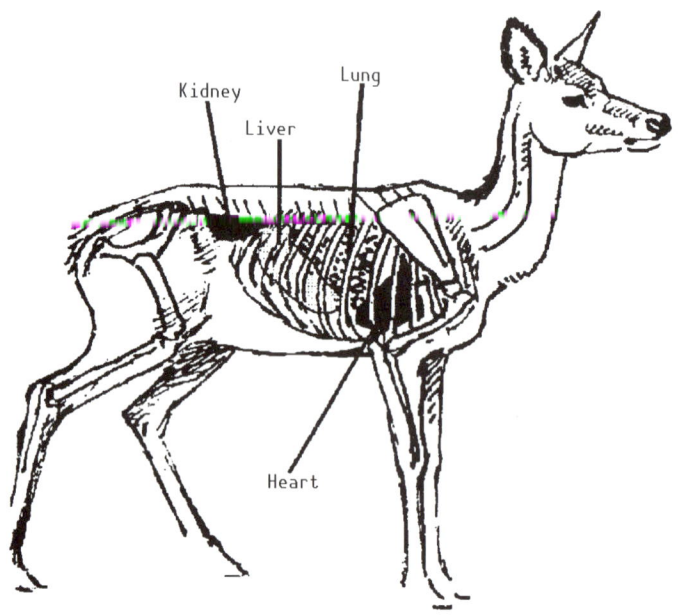

The diagram shows the position of the vital organs in a red deer hind. The layout is precisely the same for a roe, or any other deer. It can be seen that if the animal is standing broadside the ideal point of aim is in line with the back of the front leg and about a third to one half way up the body. A good guide is to follow up the back of a front leg with the rifle sight and shoot when half way up the body, for a high heart shot.

The next stage is to recognise the reaction and signs that indicate a bullet strike in different parts of the anatomy. If a shot is too far back it is often the sound, of a hollow plop, as the bullet strikes the stomach, that gives the indication of a poor shot. With such a gut shot the animal may run off a short distance and then stand hunched up, or lie down, or it may simply remain standing in the same spot, hunched up.

It is difficult to describe adequately the noise of a bullet strike in a successful target area, but with experience one learns to differentiate. The reaction of a shot animal is often the best guide to the initial indication of the area hit. A beast shot through the lungs or heart will most often run, maybe 50 or even sometimes 100 yards, before dropping dead. The heart shot run is a characteristic low to the ground dash before it collapses. Sometimes it will run in a semi-circle rather than a straight rush, especially in woodland, and sometimes the animal will not run at all but merely stand briefly before collapsing. A heart shot beast may also occasionally rear up on its hind legs and then collapse dead. The straight headlong low dash is the most usual reaction however. A somewhat similar reaction may occur with a lung shot, perhaps with the animal running a little further before dropping. A high heart shot, with the bullet damaging the major blood vessels at the top of the heart, usually results in the animal dropping where it stands. Thus the advice to aim approximately half way up the body from the belly line following up the back of the foreleg in a broadside stance, as the heart position on the diagram shows. A liver shot will also result in the animal dropping, but as well as obviously damaging the liver it may also spoil some back meat if rather high or make a mess of the guts if low, and cannot be a recommended shot.

As the diagram clearly shows, the target position of the top of the animal's heart offers the largest lethal area to ensure a humane kill, and there should be no necessity to take other shots under most circumstances. As already mentioned, despite claims that the neck shot is the preferable one because it damages no saleable meat and the animal drops instantly, most stalkers should avoid taking such a shot save in exceptional circumstances. It is worth reiterating and stressing that there are two reasons for this. The first is that the actual vital area of neck, the vertebrae, of even a red deer stag, is a very small target, and of a tiny roe deer is even smaller. This can be confirmed by taking the trouble to examine the actual neck of a deer by dissection, noting that the vertebrae do not run straight up the middle of the neck the whole way. The heart area offers a much bigger and more sensible target area. The second reason is that although the neck shot animal drops instantly, death may not be instant, as can be detected by eye movement.

A lesson that a stalker should learn is that when he has fired at a deer and apparently killed it successfully, he should always automatically load a fresh round into the rifle ready for a second shot if necessary. Something may have gone wrong and the animal may not be completely dead, so it should always be approached with caution, ready for a quick second shot if necessary. Whilst this necessity may be rare, it is by no means unknown for a deer to drop at the shot, apparently completely dead, and for the stalker to be surprised and horrified to see the animal get up and run off as he approaches. If the bullet has gone too high and merely bruised the spine, thus knocking the animal down, once recovered and on its feet again it may never be found after it has run off. So, it should be a rule that all ostensibly dead animals should still be approached after the shot as if they are potentially not dead.

A final point relevant to the actual shooting of a deer is the knowledge and experience of what are described in old venery terms as the 'paint and pins'. These are the blood and hair respectively, shed by the animal as a result of the bullet strike. All stalkers should be able to recognise some of the basic aspects of these important clues, so vital in woodland stalking, where a deer may vanish into undergrowth after being fired at, but also important from time to time on the open hill. It is easy for stalkers of red deer on open ground to ignore this aspect, believing that they can see deer well and will be able to watch them after a shot. Often this is not the case, however, and a beast may have to move only a few yards to be in dead ground from the stalker. If a deer is fired at and then vanishes, it is important that the stalker should look for signs of a hit at the exact spot where the animal stood when the shot was fired, to establish not only whether it was a hit or a miss, but to try to determine in which part of the anatomy of the beast the bullet struck.

Again, experience with not only examining carcasses hanging in the larder, but actual skinning and butchering of these, will teach a stalker the type of hair that grows in different parts of the body, for instance. The three obvious types of paint or blood to look for are the dark red blood of a heart shot, the pink frothy blood of a lung shot, and the dark messy blood containing other bits of stomach content that denotes a gut shot. Tiny fragments of bone may be found, indicating perhaps, from the shape of these, that the bullet hit a leg. Long hair may indicate that this came from the upper part of the body, and short hair probably indicates that this came from underneath the animal. It is surprising how difficult a big stag can be to find on occasions, when lying dead on an apparently open hillside. He only has to fall into a ditch or peat hag to disappear completely, and long heather can easily render a search difficult. A roe deer, in comparison, is tiny, and when lying flat can be almost invisible even in open grass, let alone in woodland cover. To start the search with an idea of where the animal was hit, and the knowledge of the likely outcome of such a wound, coupled with the possibility of a directional guide from a blood trail, is obviously likely to make the task of finding the deer easier, and to avoid the inexcusable mistake of simply assuming a miss, should the animal run off apparently unscathed, without making absolutely certain of this. Many assumed misses are subsequently found not to have been misses at all and a dead beast discovered later, or, worse, a wounded one.

The stalker, particularly in woodland or cover, should learn to look for marks of blood, even tiny drops, on leaves or grass, and by finding subsequent spots of this to follow the trail taken by a hit deer. Even when a dog is present that can find the dead beast quickly, it is still good discipline to look for a blood trail to maintain the training to do so, in order that this can be undertaken should no dog be available, or in case the dog follows the line of another deer or is distracted by rabbit scent. On open hill a beast can easily disappear rapidly into dead ground, and discovering signs of a bullet strike and a trail can indicate the direction taken.

Red Deer Stalking

In Britain by far the most red deer are stalked upon the open hill in the Highlands of Scotland. There are a handful of deer forest areas in the north of England, and red deer in woodland in the west country, Norfolk, the Lake district, and a few other places, but stalking in these areas tends to be limited and specialised, and the circumstances are mostly quite different from the ones pertaining to the conventional Scottish deer forest on which these comments concentrate.

The great majority of the people who stalk red deer in Scotland do so as guests, paying or otherwise, or clients, of either the estates that own the forest or of the agent who has leased the stalking for sub-letting to clients, possibly taken out on the hill by himself if not by the estate stalker. It is important that these guests or clients understand that they must obey the instructions of the professional stalker taking them out, just as they should obey the keeper on a pheasant shoot (in the absence, but sometimes in the presence, of his employer). This does not necessarily mean that the instructions should always be regarded as the correct ones or that one has always to agree with the stalkers, since these vary considerably in knowledge and expertise in deer matters, but rather that there might be extenuating circumstances of which the client may be unaware. However, most professional stalkers know more about the deer than most clients are ever likely to know, and they have the vital knowledge and experience of the ground gained from daily familiarity with this. Only when one has stalked a particular place in most of the combinations of the factors of wind and weather and so on can one claim to know the ground.

Nevertheless, there have been massive advances in the knowledge of deer in the past twenty years, arising directly from the proliferation of deer farming. This development has not only allowed close study of deer, but has also provided commercial incentive to fund research. Deer farming is no longer merely an unusual sideline, but is now an important and growing commercial operation in some parts of the world, and the table below demonstrates this with some example figures.

Deer farmed, mostly for venison but some for antler velvet. (Mainly red deer, but including some fallow and other species.)

New Zealand	1,400,000
China	1,000,000
Russia	400,000
USA	250,000
Australia	180,000
Germany	150,000
Korea	112,000
Canada	98,000
Mauritius	60,000
England	50,000
Eire	38,000
Taiwan	36,000
Sweden	35,000
Denmark	30,000
France	30,000

Knowledge obtained by the close study of red deer as a result of the development of commercial farming interest has debunked a number of traditional stalkers' beliefs as myths, and as a result has somewhat changed some management perspectives. We now understand better the development of antlers, the feeding and appetite cycles of deer, the hormonal influences upon them, rutting behaviour of stags, the oestrus cycle and gestation period of hinds, and so on.

One of the old traditions that has been shown to be without foundation is the idea that a hummel stag is a genetic trait like that of polled cattle and sheep and will breed hummels. It is now understood that antler generation is precipitated by hormonal function, and this in turn is influenced by feeding in a young calf, as well as by photoperiod.

If the condition of the calf is poor during the early part of its life, perhaps from insufficient milk from the hind or poor quality solid feed, so that it fails to achieve the requisite weight level after its first few months, the first flush of testosterone may be absent or insufficient to initiate proper pedicle growth, or later the development of antlers on the pedicle site. This causes the hummel condition. However the ability to grow antlers remains even though this initial catalyst was absent, and if the pedicle of a hummel is wounded or nicked an antler will grow, and moreover thereafter the antler will in due course shed and re-grow normally, since the hummel, if entire, and not castrated or with damaged testicles, will be capable of subsequent testosterone secretion, which is what influences antler growth, hardening and shedding. If one pedicle is nicked an antler will grow on that side, and if both are wounded then both will grow antlers normally in future.

That the influence of testosterone results in antler growth has been demonstrated by the implantation of this hormone into a young hind, which subsequently grew antlers. Many experiments have been carried out by researchers in order to better understand the growth of these bone structures. Whilst testosterone is the hormone responsible for the initial antler growth in the young deer, thereafter it becomes the factor in ceasing antler growth and causing the bone to harden and the velvet to dry and shrivel. The hard antler remains in situ until the testicles regress in spring and the level of testosterone drops, resulting in the casting of the antler. The wound caused by this casting initiates regrowth of the next antler. Experiments have shown that the growth of even quite large stag antlers are not a major drain on the animal's metabolism or its energy intake, and that the necessary materials are easily supplied by the food consumed in summer. Testosterone is responsible also for the other male breeding characteristics, and hinds injected with this hormone have been recorded as not only subsequently growing antlers as a result, but also roaring and mounting other hinds.

Hummels have been thought by some people to be incapable of breeding. This is not so. Indeed a hummel was used as one of the stock stags at Glensaugh, the first experimental deer farm, in Kincardineshire. All his male progeny were antlered. The old tradition that hummels seen on a deer forest must be shot was based on the idea that either they would breed other hummels, or that they are incapable of breeding, and so undesirable if they drove antlered stags from hinds. Very often hummels are large beasts, though this is not always so and research has shown that there are hummels of all sizes, just the same as with antlered stags. It may seem strange that an antler-less stag is capable of defeating a large antlered beast. This probably arises as a result of dominance in pecking order achieved during the summer. For during the summer months when stags are growing their antlers, which are still in velvet, with sensitive growing points, the hummel has the advantage of not having these sensitive growths on his head and so is able to dominate antlered stags. Furthermore, lacking these growing antlers he is not so tormented by flies on the growing points and thus is able to concentrate more upon feeding rather than retiring to the cooling breezes on the hill tops or into dark woods where flies are less abundant. This is undoubtedly why some hummels are able to become large beasts of heavy body weights.

Contrary to tradition, there is clearly some merit in the policy of leaving large hummels as breeding stock, since if they are obviously heavy animals they have demonstrated their ability to grow well despite a possible poor start in life. At the same time there could be some merit in the view that large stags that rut early, and are run and in poor condition by the middle of October, when most hinds on the hill first come into season, might well be shot if the trophy is the objective, since these are unlikely to be of much breeding use. In fact, on most deer forests where stags are abundant it is likely that a particular stag, however dominant, probably does not actually get to serve many individual hinds. Most mating takes place at night, and so if several hinds in a group are in oestrus simultaneously it is difficult for the master stag, who may be attending one of these hinds, to prevent other stags coming in to serve other hinds.

The practical results of theoretical management are difficult to demonstrate on most deer forests, and there is little evidence of the efficacy of success in improving herds over the past century. Examination of records, and antler collections, suggest that the spectrum of heads now is much the same as it has always been. This is because, although genetic influence is undoubtedly important, food supply, shelter and disturbance are even more so. This does not mean that there is any justification for necessarily altering management ideals, since these can be justified on aesthetic grounds. However, as deer farms have amply demonstrated, food has the major influence on body weight and antlers. Deer caught in the wild and introduced into deer farms with abundant food have been transformed, and poor stags and switches have become 12 pointers and more within two years or less, and achieved weights that would have been completely unattainable in the wild. However many people feel that the wild Scottish Highland red deer are more graceful animals than their massive woodland conspecifics further south, or farmed deer.

Nevertheless, in all groups of animals some do better than others, and some suffer illness or mishaps of one type or another, and there is undoubted merit in concentrating culling on these poorer animals. The problem is that some of the poor quality may be due to the dam and not to the sire, and in any case it is unlikely that in practice there will actually be any knowledge as to whether a so-called master stag has successfully served any hinds, or how many, let alone which these might be and which are his offspring. Consequently the choice of which stags to cull and which to leave is largely based upon the aesthetic ideal of keeping the best and shooting the poor ones, in the expectation and hope that the better stags will have greater procreation influence.

Antlers are amazing growths, unique to deer, being bone, not horn as with other ungulates, and being shed annually and re-grown. Under ideal conditions the annual antler growth of red deer stags tends to get progressively larger for the first few years. It is a little difficult to be specific, since under conditions of ad libitum quality food a stag can produce a large twelve point pair of antlers in his second year, whereas a wild stag in Scotland probably produces little more than a single spike on each side as his first set of antlers during his second summer. With plenty of good feeding a wild stag can then produce an eight, or even ten point head in his third year, but with poor conditions he may never produce a head as good as this. Mostly the size of antlers shows correlation with body weight, but one can get a comparatively small stag with very fine antlers on occasion, and one can also find a very heavy stag with poor antlers. Nevertheless, more usually the red deer antlers improve in quality over the first five years or so.

There can also be periods of regression too, because a stag with a royal, or twelve point, head can be seen with a much poorer ten or even eight point head, or worse, in a subsequent year, and then possibly return again to a good set of antlers in the following year. This occurs when for some reason the feeding has been poor, for instance if the stag has perhaps had trouble with his teeth and found eating difficult for a period, or been ill for a while during the summer period of growth. In his classic book "Some Account of Jura Red deer", one of the most impressive books ever written on red deer, privately published over a century ago, Henry Evans wrote that it is not easy to judge the age of indifferent stags on the hoof after about five years old, and that "There are many stags that never grow larger than a fairly good five year old animal. Arm chair judgement is much easier than hill judgement". He describes a known young stag that spent two years as a knobber and then produced a six point head, and observed that such was "A somewhat awkward fact for the cock-sure division of observers!".

During the period of growth the stag's antlers are more brittle and susceptible to damage than later when they have hardened and cleaned. Such damage may result from problems with fences or other such accidents, since the stags avoid fighting with these antlers whilst they are in velvet because the growing points are sensitive. If one examines an antler half way through growth it can be seen and felt that the bone is quite hard under the velvet except at the tips of the points, where growth is taking place. These points are warmer and the blood carrying the bone growth ingredients concentrates there, and so do the tormenting flies. Whilst still in velvet, but fully grown and close to shedding, the antlers of a large stag can appear very impressive; the size being exaggerated by the velvet. It can be noted, when comparing antlers in velvet, that the colour of this velvet can vary somewhat from light grey to dark grey or almost dark brown.

The growing of velvet, and indeed the neogenesis of hair follicles after birth, is unique to deer, as is the growing and casting annually of the strange bone tissue on their heads, the antlers.

The mechanism of the growth of antler has been well researched now. It is clear that the hormone influencing growth of the antler is initially melatonin. This is produced by the pineal gland in the brain in response to darkness, so that more melatonin is produced at night, and during the longer nights, and little is produced during the long days and short nights of midsummer. Melatonin encourages the secretion of testosterone, largely from the testicles, and this in turn precipitates antler hardening and velvet shedding, as well as the growth of a mane and rutting behaviour. Antler growth is encouraged at the time of least melatonin secretion. It has been demonstrated that by keeping stags in a completely enclosed environment with artificial light that can be manipulated to emulate waxing and waning day length, so controlling the photoperiodic influence, the growth of the antlers can be adjusted. By exposing stags to three artificial periods of waxing and waning day length during one year they can be induced to grow and cast three sets of antlers in the year.

With wild stags the present day value is in the antlers, commercially assessed on a trophy basis, and although on most forests stags with very good heads are usually preserved and not allowed to be shot, on some estates the stags are specially fed and large trophies subsequently sold at high prices. Although fine antler trophies have always been cherished, only in the last century and a half, since deer stalking became a commercialised sport, have these taken precedence over the value of the venison. In times past high quality venison was the objective of the chase or hunt. Roe deer were not regarded as choice meat since these do not lay down fat like red deer. *The Master of Game*, the first book on hunting in English, quoted that "The roebuck hath no season to be hunted, for they bear no venison...." These days venison is advertised with the selling point that it is lean meat, but this is largely because farmed venison is sold young, before fat is laid down, and wild venison is rarely shot in best condition. A century ago many deer forests ceased stalking stags by October 12th or earlier, since the rut is mostly in full swing by then, and rutting stags use up so much energy, combined with limited feeding, that they can lose up to a third of their body weight during this period. Run stags were not considered worth shooting.

In early centuries the main season for hunting stags was when they were 'in pride of grease' and had laid down fat in summer, and when the quality of the venison was the best, which was from midsummer until the end of September. In his book *English Deer Parks* Shirley states that the time of the fallow buck season, or the grease or fat season (tempus pinguedinis) was between August 1st and Holyrood Day, September 14th. There is no doubt that the best venison comes from a young stag, in perhaps his third or fourth year when he has finished growing, and at the end of the summer, during which he has laid down fat as a result of good feeding, but before the start of rutting behaviour. Early September is therefore the ideal time for shooting a stag for venison. An alternative might be a fat yeld hind at the start of the hind season, but these probably begin to lose condition with being harried in the rut coupled with falling autumnal food quality.

A few estates start stag stalking in the summer in order to obtain better quality venison, and to take advantage of the higher price paid then by dealers for these better quality carcasses, and if poor antlered beasts are being shot, where the heads are of little trophy value anyway, there is merit in a policy of starting the stag stalking early to make a start towards achieving target cull stag numbers. From the stalking viewpoint the stags may still be further out on the forest, on high ground, but the stalk should be just as exciting, and the weather possibly more favourable.

For the majority of stalkers of red deer the rut is the most exciting time of the year. In many places stags are not often seen at all in summer. On lower hind ground, or in lowland wooded areas, stags spend much of the summer trying to avoid the torment of flies and midges on their growing antlers, and so resort to the high tops of the hills where there is a breeze to keep off these pests, or perhaps the temperature is sufficiently cool for them to be absent, or else the stags retire into thick dark woods to escape them, emerging to feed at night when these insects are not around. Some time after midsummer, perhaps as a result of the catalyst of the solstice and the change to shortening days, testosterone secretion in the stags increases. This has the effect of making the animal's mane grow, and for his neck to thicken, and it also results in the hardening of the stag's antlers and the drying and peeling of the velvet from these. As well as the mane growing and the neck hair lengthening, the whole pelage changes to the darker winter coat. The hairs on the penis sheath also lengthen and the stag urinating in a spraying motion, often over its own belly, causes these to blacken and become smelly. The thicker, hollow, winter hairs grow imperceptibly through the thin summer coat, perhaps doubling, or more, the total hair numbers. The existing summer pelage hairs also lengthen and become hollow and lower down, at the base of the hairs, appear indistinguishable from the new winter ones, although they retain their red tips, which gives the stag's winter coat the red flecked appearance. Most literature refers to the summer pelage being moulted when the winter coat grows, but the stalker will find no evidence of this in wallows or places where the deer have been lying, or negotiating fences. Deer do not moult in autumn.

Many stalkers seem to regard the rut itself, manifested by stags roaring and fighting, as the actual mating season, as evidenced by reports that the rut was over in some area by the end of the stag season on October 20th, or was over very early in the season. Some have even suggested that the roaring of the stags is a catalyst to prompt the hinds to come into season. At this time of year stags can travel great distances in search of hinds. This active searching is referred to as 'breaking out': that is, leaving the summer bachelor groups of stags to go off in search of mates. A stag can easily travel twenty miles in a night in search of hinds. Often a travelling stag will be accompanied by a smaller stag, known as his fag, or squire.

Stags come into season mostly in late September and traditionally September 22nd, the autumn equinox, is known as 'The Day of the Roaring' in the Gaelic calendar; but the actual flush of testosterone is idiosyncratic and some stags can come into season and start searching for hinds in August, whilst others may not take much interest until late October. Once a stag is in season, secreting testosterone and ready to mate, he remains in this state for a couple of months or more. In other words he remains in season and able to mate throughout the period, unlike the hind, who cycles every eighteen to twenty-one days until successfully served, and may be able to conceive for only a very short period, perhaps a few hours, during the appropriate stage of the cycle. However, the stag loses up to a third of his body weight during rutting, and becomes so worn out and in such poor condition that his ability to get the opportunity to mate is much reduced by then. With farmed deer, a mature stag can successfully serve fifty hinds, but in the wild any stag is unlikely to serve properly more than a handful of hinds. This is because of the competition and activity.

When a stag comes into season and finds hinds, he attempts to hold these in some suitable area where he may be able to see off rivals. In the early part of the rut, when few, or no, hinds have yet come into season, the stag expends much energy herding these, constantly on the lookout for a mate that might become receptive. At this time of the year the stag's appetite is considerably reduced. This, coupled with the activity involved in trying to keep his group of prospective mates together, and chasing off any rivals that appear, results in the rapid loss of his body weight, perhaps over as little as a three week period. Early in the stag season one can see these beasts 'holding' a group of hinds, trying to keep them together, and away from rivals, roaring and constantly on the move rounding up their harem. All this activity is largely the result of frustration, being themselves in a state of high sexual excitement but not finding any hinds receptive. Once a hind comes into season the stag concentrates upon serving her for the brief period that she remains receptive. After the period of about three weeks at the end of October and the beginning of November, when the majority of hinds have been served and conceived, most stags, by then in lower condition and having lost much weight, and with less incentive to remain with the hinds, drift off back to their more usual haunts; though a few younger stags, as well as staggies, remain with the hinds until at least late winter.

Both stags and hinds have a second period of reduced appetite, in late winter, around February and March. This is found to occur even with captive deer offered ad lib feed. It may be a mechanism to conserve energy at a time when both feed and its value is low, since reduced appetite means less movement searching for food and so less energy use. Many stags that ended their rutting period in very poor condition enter the difficult winter period at this disadvantage, and in a severe winter may suffer badly, and even die, as a result.

The Hill

Until stags 'break out' and go off in search of hinds they remain in the bachelor parties in which they spend the summer, mostly on high ground in open country. These stag parties may be small groups or quite large herds. The first stags to start to rut are generally older beasts, but not always so. It not known whether a stag that starts to rut early does so each season, or whether he may rut early one season and rather later another, but the trait is probably idiosyncratic and a stag that reacts earlier to the hormone induced stimuli probably does so consistently.

Red deer are largely crepuscular or nocturnal animals, and mostly they tend to move down onto lower ground and better feeding at night, returning to higher ground with daylight. Although the rutting stag tries to keep his chosen harem together in a small area, if the lead hind decides to move off, the stag has little option but to follow the group. Although the deer do feed during the day time, their main feeding period is probably at night and much of the day is spent resting, and so they are attracted to places that offer shelter from prevailing wind and weather in which to spend the day. Wind is an extremely important factor affecting all deer, and is especially important in their choice of where to spend the day.

Stalkers soon discover the difficulty of determining wind flow in the hills. This can be most deceiving. If one observes domestic livestock in fields on a windy day one often sees a group of cows or a flock of sheep seemingly sheltering in front of trees or some other obstacle apparently in full face of the wind. The reason for this is that the wind, or air current, rises to clear the obstacle, leaving a sheltered patch where this rises over it. The same phenomenon can occur on the hill. Corries and burns are especially difficult to assess in wind, since sometimes the air current can be found perversely moving in the opposite of the anticipated direction. In these circumstances the experience of a stalker who has tried approaches to such a position in all wind directions and weather conditions is of vital importance to the success of a stalk. Deer are familiar with wind vagaries and seem to take full advantage of it. They usually lie with the wind at their backs facing down wind, so that they can keep a watchful eye open for danger coming up wind, and relying upon scent to be carried from behind them.

It is difficult to estimate how far the stalker's scent can be carried upon the wind, because circumstances vary so much, but it must be assumed that with a steady breeze over flat ground deer could smell a human at up to a mile distance. Their reaction at long range to human scent may well depend upon how accustomed they are to the smell. Over broken ground, with a gusty wind, the scent might well be dispersed at a much shorter distance; but caution in this respect is wise. Nothing is more frustrating to a stalker than after achieving apparently successfully a long arduous stalking manoeuvre to find that on reaching the firing point the deer have vanished.

Because of their reliance upon scent for guarding against unseen approach of danger, deer do not like very strong or gusty wind and become noticeably unsettled in these conditions. Undoubtedly they find exposure to strong wind uncomfortable, as do most creatures, but quite probably in such circumstances scent may get broken up or somewhat dispersed in some way and so become a less reliable protection. In woodland there is no doubt that the noise of the wind in the trees also unsettles the deer, making their hearing less reliable.

As deer are equipped with a large olfactory organ, so they are also provided with large ears, which they use with great proficiency. Their ears operate independently and they can swivel these individually towards sounds. On the open hill, especially in windy conditions, the acuteness of the hearing of red deer may be less apparent, but observation of the animals in a more sheltered situation soon establishes just how good is their hearing. In particular stalkers must avoid sounds that are completely out of place in the environment, such as metallic noises made by a rifle bolt for instance, or a stick upon a rock.

Although deer in Britain have no predators, other than foxes and eagles killing their young, they are essentially prey animals, designed for awareness and flight. They have large eyes, situated on the sides of their heads, which is the position of the eyes of prey animals that need as much all round vision as possible, rather than at the front like predatory animals, including humans, that concentrate their sight on objects of pursuit. Deer have excellent eyesight, and rely upon this sense for protection and awareness as much as their other senses. Experience on the hill soon shows that deer have good long sight as well as the ability to pick up movement rapidly. Sometimes, on the open hill, red deer seem not to bother with humans that they can surely see at long range, when they feel that no danger threatens. This may cause some people to doubt their long range sight ability. However, once disturbed and alert it becomes clear just how well they can see. Their long sight is certainly as good as, if not better than, that of humans.

In the past there has been debate as to what degree of colour can be distinguished by deer, and indeed by other animals. In recent years work has been carried out in America researching the eyesight of White-tailed and fallow deer. What we perceive as colour, interpreted as such by our brain, is light of differing wavelengths reflected from objects. There are effectively three light wavelengths interpreted as colours. Short wavelength is seen as blue, medium wavelength as green, and long wavelength light is red. All colours are a combination of these three. As far as is known, only primates amongst mammals have what is called trichromatic vision, or the ability to see all three wavelengths. This is because only primates are known to possess the necessary three types of photoreceptors. Deer have only two of them. Birds, or certainly some species of them, are thought to be able to see all three colour ranges.

The retina in the back of the eye of mammals is composed of two types of light receptors, rods and cones. Rods are the receptors used in very poor light conditions or in darkness. Research has found that deer have more rods in their eyes than humans, and so their vision in poor light is better. A further aid to their eyesight in poor light is that their eyes are large and their pupils open wider, letting in more light. Also they have a membraneous reflecting layer of cells in the choroid, or vascular, part of the back of their eyes, called a tapetum. This acts as a sort of mirror, reflecting back any light not absorbed initially by the receptor cells, so enabling the animals to make maximum use of what light is available.

This tapetum is identified in those nocturnal or crepuscular animals that have it by the fact that the eyes shine in the light of a torch or spotlight. Humans do not possess a tapetum and their eyes do not shine in torch light.

The eyes of deer contain fewer cones than humans however, and these are the photoreceptors used in daytime vision for the reception of light of differing wavelengths. As mentioned, research has shown that deer possess only two types of cones, those receptive to short and medium wavelengths. They lack the cones receptive to long wavelength, or red colours. Thus deer have colour vision limited to the blue and green sections of the spectrum. The indications are that they may have poorer daytime sight than humans by reason of the fewer cones, but this is not borne out by observations of wild deer. Of course, one can only interpret what is presumed about deer eyesight in terms of human experience and extrapolate accordingly. Human eyes apparently have a filter that blocks most ultraviolet light at the very low end of the wavelength spectrum. This helps to reduce glare and enable more sharp focusing. It seems that deer do not possess this filter against ultraviolet light. Perhaps their larger eyes help to mitigate against this?

The problem of walkers and 'Munro-baggers' on the hills, in deer forests, is not new, and there have been records of stalks spoiled by walkers as far back as the last century; but the situation has worsened enormously over the past twenty years, and seems to continue to do so annually. Deer are disturbed both by seeing and by winding walkers, and can move considerable distances as a result of such disturbance.

A 'Munro' is a Scottish mountain that is over 3000 feet (914 metres) in height, so called after Sir Hugh Thomas Munro, who published a list of these, as long ago as 1891, in the Journal of the Scottish Mountaineering Club. This shows that even a century ago there were keen hillwalkers! There are now maps, charts, and even computer software, showing the location of the 277 Munros listed, and even the 221 Corbetts, which are hills in a list published by J.R. Corbett that are over 2500 feet (760 metres). Moreover a Percy Donald produced a list of hills over 2000 feet (610 metres) which are now known as Donalds. Consequently there are few Scottish deer forests without a Munro, Corbett or Donald on their ground, and the risk of ardent walkers wishing to add the visiting of these to their list of triumphs.

Although deer apparently get used to walkers in some areas, and appear to take little notice of them, there can be no doubt that the animals are nevertheless alerted by the awareness of humans in their vicinity and consequently more wary and likely to shift position.

Red deer are more wandering than sedentary animals when given the opportunity. They may have a range that they frequent, but they prefer to wander through this, choosing food of different types in different places if they can, and resting in places where conditions suit them. This wandering as they feed is perhaps seen more readily in woodland deer. On the open hill the feeding areas may be restricted, both by wind and weather and appropriate shelter, and by the availability of suitable grazing and browsing, which may be concentrated in green areas around springs and burn sides. So red deer on the hill may tend to spend much of the day in one place, coming off the hill to feed on lower ground at night; but with a change in the wind they may well decide to move, perhaps to another part of the hill, or even to a different, more sheltered corrie or hillside. Stags are very much more prone to wandering, and it is mainly stags that maraud into farm crops and agricultural land in winter, and mostly stags that come to feed put out for the deer in winter.

The roaring of stags at rutting time is sometimes referred to in parts of England as belling, a derivative of bellowing. the red deer noise most familiar to stalkers, but the hinds can be quite vociferous at times. If one observes within ear-shot an area where the deer come down in the evening to feed in numbers one can generally hear various calls between hinds and calves, and sometimes from stags too. A hind calling a calf can give a noise rather like a yelp or squeak, which appears to carry a surprisingly long way. On the other hand a hind that is disturbed suddenly, or perturbed but a little uncertain, perhaps having glimpsed a stalker at close range, may give a deep resonant bark, like someone striking hard an empty 40 gallon oil drum with a large stick.

The roaring of stags appears to be a hormonally induced reaction. Although an occasional roar can sometimes be heard on the hill even as late as December, mostly it has ceased by about mid November, and in some areas it is often mostly finished before that. Experiments with hormonal treatment, or changes to photoperiod or daylight length, have been shown to induce early roaring in line with early velvet shedding and antler hardening, and the presence of hinds is not necessary to precipitate this.

Roaring takes place in different circumstances. A stag 'breaking out', or going off to search for hinds, prompted by a flush of testosterone, will often stop to roar occasionally whilst travelling. This may be to solicit a response from another stag that may be holding hinds, in order to locate these, or it may merely be an almost involuntary manifestation of the hormonal driven urge to mate. A stag that has already taken charge of some hinds will stand and roar if he sees another male deer, a potential rival, and this certainly appears to be a defiant challenge or a warning to the intruder. In some species of animals the beast making the loudest noise is usually the dominant one. For instance it is thought that amongst horses the stallion with the loudest scream is likely to be the dominant one, since the superior sound suggests better lungs and a larger healthier owner of these. However, defeated and 'run' stags will still roar. It is not uncommon to see a dark stag, with tucked up belly, obviously in poor condition having lost a great deal of weight and well run after the rut, lying by himself roaring, to nobody in particular, but doing so as an instinctive reaction.

Bearing in mind that the stags mostly come into season, flushed with testosterone, two or three weeks before the majority of hinds start their oestrus cycle, it would seem likely that roaring, as well as aggression to other males, and the constant chivvying of hinds, keeping these together and checking for signs of oestrus, are manifestations of frustration at failing to find a receptive hind.

Culmination of the Stalk

After making a shot at a deer it is important to reload the rifle quickly and be prepared to take a second shot in case of some unforeseen circumstance. Even if the beast has fallen apparently dead as anticipated, it is wise to observe it for a few moments to ensure that this is the case. The animal should then be approached cautiously, with the rifle ready for action and not returned to its cover, until it is completely certain that it is dead. Accidents have occurred following the stag merely being knocked down but not killed, as a result of the bullet going too high, and then recovering to rise to its feet and make off when the stalker is about to handle it for gralloching. Many stalkers test the beast by touching its eye with the end of rifle barrel or knife to confirm that there is no reflex movement.

It is important for the quality of the venison that the blood is drained from the animal as quickly as possible. Bleeding the animal also needs to be carried out rapidly after death before the blood coagulates. This is done by inserting the point of the knife into the base of the throat and back into the chest to cut the large blood vessels above the heart. When this is done dark blood should flow freely from the wound, draining the chest cavity of much of the blood. This procedure is not necessary with woodland deer or where the animal is shot in a place from which transport is simple and no dragging is required, because in such a situation it is preferable to remove all the viscera, including heart and lungs, in order for the whole body cavity to be exposed and ensure cooling of the carcass as rapidly as possible.

Where the animal has to be dragged, or transported a long distance, a Highland gralloch is more customary. This involves leaving the diaphragm intact and not removing the heart and lungs. In this case the idea is to make as small an incision as convenient for removing the stomach and intestines in order to expose the minimum body cavity to the dragging process, and because it is easier to carry the heart and lungs back inside the beast. The liver and kidneys may be left inside the carcass too, or removed and carried separately in a plastic bag.

Gralloching is made easier if a second person can hold the legs of the deer, but if alone the stalker should set the beast on its back, standing between the hind legs to keep these apart. If the animal is a stag, then the penis sheath should be grasped with one hand and cut off with the knife in the other hand, lifting this to cut the skin with the knife horizontal to the body cavity to avoid puncturing this. The penis and testicles should be cut off in one piece, severing the penis near the anus, cutting off only the outer skin in the process and not piercing the body cavity membrane. The latter should then be grasped carefully at a point near the pelvis and lifted whilst a small incision is made with the knife point large enough to enable two finger tips to be inserted. The knife point can then be inserted between these finger tips in an almost horizontal position, with the fingers acting as a shield to prevent the point of the knife cutting any of the viscera below. In this manner the knife can be run up the length of the belly to make a sufficient opening in this to enable removal of the required organs. To make a good job of cleaning the animal and avoid the possibility of spilling any gut contents inside the body cavity, some stalkers then tie a small piece of string round the alimentary canal at the upper end, either at the gullet, or where this emerges through the diaphragm, depending on the extent of the gralloch, to avoid spillage of the contents where the cut is made, and also at the lower end where this enters the pelvic arch. The stomach and intestines can then be drawn out to one side, carefully severing any connective tissue and avoiding piercing organs with the knife.

The rectum must then be removed, by cutting around this from the rear, external, end. It is safe to cut all round this since the pelvic arch will preclude damaging the haunch meat. When freed, the end of the alimentary passage can be grasped and pulled gently out. It will probably then be seen that beside this, in the pelvic arch, lies the bladder, which may well contain urine. This is best released by gently cutting connective tissue from inside, enabling both the rectum and the bladder to be pulled out from the internal side of the pelvic arch.

When gralloching a deer it is wise to be observant for abnormalities and signs of disease or parasitic infection, for knowledge of the well-being of the herd. Lesions in the lungs or liver are possible aberrations that may be noticed. Many deer, especially in the north and west of Scotland, suffer from liver fluke infestation. Pale areas or lesions in the liver may indicate something wrong, and a check for fluke can be easily made by cutting open one of the major bile ducts, which converge into a hard grisly junction of tubes at the top of the liver. If liver flukes are present in numbers some of the adult form of these flat leaf-like creatures, about the size of a finger nail, can be squeezed from the bile ducts. One of the features of Cervids (which include our deer species in this country) is that they do not possess a gall bladder, with the exception of the Musk deer. Those familiar with dressing poultry will be aware of the necessity of cutting out the gall bladder from the livers of geese and chickens before use. Another Cervid distinguishing feature is the possession of double lachrymal orifices, seen in the depressed gland below the eye on each side of the face, which secrets a substance that is sometimes used in scent marking.

In some circumstances it may be necessary to leave the carcass for collection later, especially if it is the aim to shoot several beasts during the day. It may be prudent in an area where eagles are plentiful, as in the north-west Highlands for instance, to safeguard the carcass from damage by these, and also to render the beast easily seen by whomsoever is to collect it later, by tying a white plastic bag to the antlers or to a leg. Eagles will frequently descend upon a freshly killed carcass and peck around the bullet wound, or the site of the gralloch, or remove the eyes and tongue, and in some cases make a terrible mess of it. A fluttering plastic bag or handkerchief deters them.

If the dead animal can be collected by machine or pony from the place of gralloching the stalker is fortunate. In many cases it will necessary to move the carcass to a more accessible position, however, and in some it may be the requirement that the beast is dragged manually off the hill altogether. There are various techniques for dragging a deer; but basically there are two main points to bear in mind to make this onerous task easier. The first is that the head should be raised a little above the ground when dragging, and if it is a stag the antlers must be kept well clear of the ground to avoid entanglement with foliage or rocks. The second point is that the animal should be dragged with, and not against, the direction of the way that the hair lies, since the latter will increase friction enormously. One method is to tie a rope around the base of animal's antlers, or if it is a hind, then around her neck, and pass the rope over the top of the head and down onto the nose, making a hitch around the upper jaw. This will help to keep the head upright.

Planning the route of a drag is most important. Even with three people pulling, dragging a large red deer uphill, for instance over heather, can be a daunting and exhausting procedure. Therefore detailed knowledge of the ground is a great advantage, so that the route for dragging can be planned to allow gradual descent of the contours of the hill where necessary to avoid burns and gullies and subsequent uphill drags.

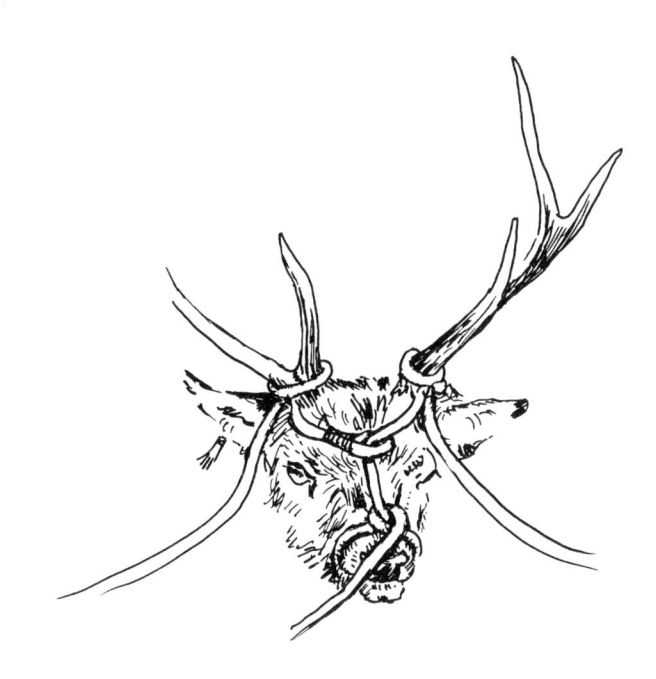

Venison in the Larder

For many stalkers the safe depositing of the deer carcass in the larder may be the culmination of their association with it. However it is of great importance that even if the butchering of the animal for their own consumption is not involved, they should at least thoroughly familiarise themselves with the anatomy of a deer. Without doubt, skinning and butchering an animal, as well as gralloching it, is vital experience in learning deer anatomy, and this should be undertaken by all stalkers at some stage, if not regularly, in order to familiarise themselves with the layout of organs and bone structures so that they can envisage these when it comes to taking a shot.

The 'trophy' is probably the first operation in the mind of the stalker, since this preparation is usually carried out soon after the stalk, whereas the venison carcass will hang perhaps for a week or more. Some people prefer to skin the skulls, or part skulls, prior to boiling these to remove the meat and tissue from the bone. However a simpler method is to boil the skull with the skin on until this commences shrinking. It will then be found that the cooked skin and meat and other tissue can be cut off the bone with ease. Well cleaned the skull becomes acceptably white when dry. Those who prefer a bleached white colour may then treat the skull; always remembering that unnatural white bone and polished antlers often look rather artificial. Household bleach may be used to whiten the bone, or Hydrogen peroxide, and even Chloride toilet cleaner may produce the desired result. One method is to use 5-10% Hydrogen peroxide, soaking rags in this and placing these on the skull, but taking care not to leave these in place too long. There is little point in going to the trouble of bleaching the skull to be pearly white if it is destined to be hung on a wall to become dusty in time.

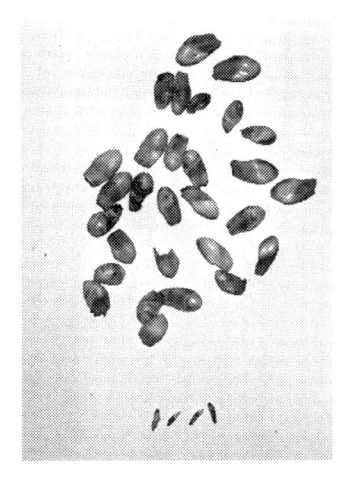

Stag tusks, with 4 roe tusks below.

A red deer trophy that is often valued by continental stalkers is the pair of vestigial canine teeth, or tusks, in the upper jaw. In an old stag these may show a brown pattern, but this is not apparent in the tusks of young beasts. At one time there was a good demand for these tusks (grandeln in German) from German jewellers and they were regarded as perquisites for the professional stalker, who was able to sell them. The tusks are easily removed from the upper jaw with a knife, since they are not attached in a socket in the same way as the conventional teeth and can readily be cut out of the gum.

The length of time that a red deer carcass should be hung before cutting this up depends upon the facility for hanging, the weather, and personal taste. In a proper temperature controlled cool room the beast may be hung for a fortnight or more, but in an ordinary outbuilding or old fashioned deer larder the weather is all important; particularly variation in temperature. Except in very cold weather, under such latter conditions a week to ten days is probably plenty of time for hanging and it may be in condition to be cut up after only five or six days if the temperature is not very cold. Whether the animal is hung in skin or already skinned again depends upon facilities and taste, but hanging in skin is probably more usual and the skin acts as a film to protect the meat.

Some people prefer to skin deer with the carcass lying upon a special skinning table. Others prefer to carry out the procedure with the carcass hanging by its hind legs. The latter is the simpler method, with the carcass hanging from a gambrel through the tendons of its hind legs. The head will already have been cut off, and the heart and lungs removed and the body cavity cleaned when the beast was originally delivered to the larder and hung up. If the front legs have not already been removed, this should now be done, cutting round the joint with a sharp knife and then twisting to break the connecting tissue. The skin of the chest should now be cut, continuing the opening made during the gralloch, right down to the end of the neck. Then the front leg skin should then be carefully slit, taking care not to cut into the meat, in a line up the back of the remaining section of leg to the opening of the chest.

Next, preferably using a proper skinning knife, although this is not necessary, the skin of the hind legs should be slit up the inside of the leg from the pelvis to the point where the gambrel is inserted. The skin at the top of the leg should then be peeled back all the way round, and gradually pulled down, easing the tissue attached to this with the skinning knife until the entire skin has been pulled down from over the back and off the neck.

The cutting up of the carcass again is subject to preferred practice. The simplest method is to cut this into two shoulders, two haunches, a neck, and a saddle and the remainder of the back. Though it may be preferred to use all the backstraps, or meat from the back including the saddle, as steak. This involves cutting all the meat from the back in two strips, which are later cut into steaks of suitable size. The filet is also removed from inside the body cavity too, of course. The haunch of a red deer stag is very large and may need to be halved for normal use and for cooking in a modern small oven.

The weights, of deer are generally recorded and reported, being of interest for comparing size and quality of animals; but a problem arises in interpreting reported weights, since the criteria are often not consistent. Much depends upon whether the carcass is completely clean or weighed including the heart and lungs, and whether the head and legs are still attached. As a rule, the killing out percentage, which is to say the butcher ready skinned carcass, works out at around 60%-65% of the animal's liveweight. The head and antlers may represent around 5% of the liveweight, and the organs generally left in the carcass with a Highland gralloch could amount also to this proportion of the liveweight or perhaps to 7%-8% of the gralloched carcass. The skin and feet might represent an amount heavier still. Thus, the stated weight of the beast might vary by perhaps 10% according to what was actually weighed, and a 14 stone stag could thus be recorded with a weight a stone heavier or lighter according to procedure.

In 1917 a Mr. R.B. Loder carefully weighed an 18 stone stag as he fell, and skinned and butchered this, recording every item as weighed. The result was the following table:-

Skin and feet	21 lbs	% total weight	8
Head and antlers	12		5
Blood	6		2
Guts and paunch	40		16
Liver, heart and lungs and windpipe	12		5
Suet	2		1
Carcass	159		63
TOTAL	252		100

Red Deer Hinds

Until quite recently hind stalking tended to be regarded partly as a cropping operation and partly a management job for the deer forest or estate. The hind cull was carried out by the estate stalkers, and its success was greatly dependent upon the weather conditions. In the Highlands of Scotland days grow short in winter, and the weather deteriorates and both cloud cover on the hills and snow and hard weather render stalking conditions difficult. There are many days during the winter when going out to stalk hinds is either impossible or unwise due to weather conditions. More recently, as the interest in deerstalking has increased, and the financial viability of estates has decreased, thus requiring more revenue producing enterprises, so some deer forests have introduced the possibility of a certain amount of commercialised hind stalking, letting days to guest rifles.

Many other estates take the view that the extra revenue available from letting out hind stalking does not compensate for the problems involved with taking out paying guests, and in particular the possible interference with the achievement of requisite cull figures. This is because the operation is invariably slowed down by taking out a guest, who is generally not so fit as the professional estate stalkers, who does not know the ground, who has to have pointed out to him or her which beasts to shoot, and whose expertise with a rifle under practical conditions may be unknown. An estate stalker or stalkers unhindered by a guest are likely to be able to cull more hinds in the comparatively few days with suitable stalking conditions, and thus able to better achieve the cull target number of hinds, at a time when estates are under pressure to not merely achieve their targets but to shoot more hinds to reduce numbers.

Hind stalking is generally regarded as poorer sport than the stalking of stags, since there is no trophy at the end of a stalk, and weather conditions are often worse, and consequent to both of these the price charged is inevitably lower. However this is a rather misplaced view. Particularly early in the hind season the weather can sometimes be at least as pleasant as in the stag season, although it invariably deteriorates later as snow falls on the hills or the weather becomes wetter and stormier. The actual stalking of hinds is just as exciting as that of stalking a stag, since the same care has to be taken and the approach is likely to be equally difficult. As a result of the high charges levied upon stag stalking, for those interested in the excitement of the actual stalk and the exhilaration of the demanding exercise is splendid scenery, rather than in acquiring an indifferent set of antlers to hang upon the wall, hind stalking probably offers better value.

Deer populations throughout much of the northern hemisphere have increased in the past two decades, including North America and some European countries. Part of the reason for this may be the result of improved habitat in the form of new forestry areas post war in some places, part due as well to conservation measures as in North America, and part perhaps due to a periodic population increase that appears to take place with some creatures. Red deer numbers in Britain generally have probably increased, though not so dramatically as in some other countries. Numbers for England are unknown, though a figure is quoted for Scotland by the Deer Commission for Scotland. Publicity by the latter, and by some conservationists with their own particular axes to grind, has given rise to the widely held opinion that red deer numbers have increased dramatically in recent years to the extent that habitat is being harmed as a result. However figures quoted by the Deer Commission for Scotland indicate that red deer numbers on the open hill have not actually increased for the past two decades, since it was reported that the Scottish red deer population was 255,000 in 1979, 300,000 in 1989, and the latest statement from the DCS in 1998 suggested a population figure of 250,000. Of course these figures are only guestimates and nobody really knows precise numbers, though the judgement of the trend is probably correct.

Hinds tend not to wander as much as stags, and also to be rather less bold, so that at places where estates feed deer it is mostly stags that come to the food, and often these are regular greedy beasts that hang around waiting for the hand-out. Hinds do not maraud onto farm land, and into gardens in winter, so frequently as the stags, and so create less problems from this view point. Nevertheless there is pressure in deer management to check hind numbers by culling annually, since it is the hinds that breed and result in increased deer numbers. So that the culling of hinds is important in the management of the deer herd.

The choice of which hinds to shoot is the subject for debate amongst stalkers. In the past, when the purpose in shooting hinds was entirely for venison, the choice was invariably to try to shoot fat yeld hinds, since being yeld, or without a calf, they were in better condition, without the burden of having to feed a calf. A hind may be yeld for a variety of reasons. Many yeld hinds will have given birth to a calf the previous summer, but will have lost this calf at some stage subsequently. Few hinds will actually be infertile and incapable of breeding. On the open hill on poor ground the survival rate of red deer calves born is possibly as low as 30%-40%, whereas in better forests this figure is likely to improve to 50%-60% or higher, and on good ground with adequate good quality feed and shelter, and on deer farms, the survival rate of calves will rise to 90%. With poorer feeding the production of milk to feed a calf can be a strain upon the metabolism of the hind, and under such circumstances a number of milk hinds will fail to conceive, and if they do so this may be later in the season than most of the hinds in good condition. So at hind stalking time their calves may be smaller. Most yeld hinds will be found to have conceived during the previous rut and be carrying an embryo, whereas some milk hinds will be found not to be pregnant.

There is a theory that hinds in good condition produce stag calves. It is unlikely that embryo sex can be influenced externally, but it is true that stag calves, and male young in many species, tend to be born bigger, and as such may find survival under harsh conditions more difficult, and so less likely with dams in poor condition. There are problems not only between the choice of whether to cull yeld or milk hinds, but also between which milk hinds to take if that is the policy. It is quite likely that a milk hind in poor condition in winter is thus as a result of concentrating the benefit of her food intake into milk for her calf, and some poor looking hinds are actually raising good calves. Similarly age may not be a judgement criterion since some old hinds continue to produce good calves for many years. On the other hand a milk hind in good condition with a poor calf may well indicate that she has been feeding herself instead of the calf and so not be good breeding stock.

The biggest problem with making such decisions is being certain as to which calves belong to which hinds in a group. This is by no means obvious, and despite confidence shown by professional stalkers in choosing the correct hind and calf pair to cull, DNA tests have shown that sometimes the confidence is misplaced. It is unlikely that time or circumstances will permit long observation before taking a shot to increase the likelihood of correctly matching hind with calf and then choosing which to cull.

The argument for culling poor calves and poor hinds is that these are less likely to survive harsh winter conditions and diseases, and that they are likely to be the poorer breeding stock. On the other hand, culling yeld hinds, which are likely to be those in best condition in a group, has three advantages. Firstly these animals are likely to be significantly heavier than milk hinds and so to produce more valuable carcasses. Secondly, where the aim is to reduce or control deer numbers the culling of yeld hinds is more likely to reduce the next generation at the same time, as evidenced by the figures from one deer forest that researched and recorded the data, which showed that 90% of the yeld hinds were in calf but 80% of the milk hinds were not in calf. Although the latter figure was probably biased by the choice of poor milk hinds for culling, research has shown that in high populations of deer on poor ground the fecundity rate of milk hinds does fall very low. Thirdly, the shooting of yeld hinds is preferable on grounds of humanity when considering the risk of failing to kill the correct calf with the hind. Some milk hinds continue to lactate until well after the hind season, and indeed for much longer than that, and depriving a calf that is still suckling of its vital milk supply is likely to reduce its chances of winter survival. Equally the unquantifiable but vital factor of what might be best described as 'motherly love' is important for a calf, especially in severe conditions, and the absence of this is again likely to have an adverse effect upon the calf.

On many, if not on most, deer forests the pressure to achieve the target cull total of hinds is such that on many stalking outings the choice of which type of hind to shoot may not arise and it may be more a question of shooting as many beasts as possible. This is unfortunate from any management viewpoint, but is the inevitable result of the pressure to shoot large numbers of hinds in limited time and weather conditions.

Stalkers are also divided in opinion on whether it is expedient to shoot the calf or the hind first. Some take the view that if the hind is shot the calf will stay near her and can then also be shot. Others may argue the other way round. If the calf is shot first it does at least eliminate the risk of leaving a disadvantaged orphan, but it also reduces venison income for the estate if the hind is not taken too. The figures published showing the annual red deer culls handled by dealers suggest that a low proportion of calves are shot each year, but this does not indicate a high bias towards killing yeld hinds, since it is far more likely that milk hinds were shot but the calves were not killed at the same time. With opinion so divided, one must allow to some degree the differing circumstances on different deer forests. Those exhorting the culling of large numbers of hinds offer little guidance to stalkers in this respect, and in a proper attempt at management of deer herds more thought should be given to the question of the emphasis on choice of which hinds to cull.

One of the reasons put forward for the culling of hinds, or of red deer generally, is that without the shooting of a number of these, especially old or poor condition animals, winter deaths would be far higher. These deaths are frequently referred to as being caused by starvation, and this is often suggested as an argument proposing that the deer population is too high. There can be no doubt that the food factor is of significance, and it has been demonstrated that in high populations of deer the mean age at death does decline and the numbers of calves dying during their first year increases significantly. Whilst the latter may be due to insufficient milk provided by a dam in poor condition, starvation may not be the direct cause of death. Animals of all kinds in poor condition, and particularly those that are weak, are highly susceptible to infection by disease and parasites; their metabolism not being in an optimum state for activating their immunity systems to best advantage.

The specific causes of deaths in wild deer have not been widely investigated, partly because in proportion to the numbers that die carcasses are rarely discovered, and partly since when corpses of deer are found, especially when in a group, these are generally described as resulting from starvation, and this is often attributed to over-population. In fact death is likely to be from a number of causes. Not least, where several dead deer are found together, is the hazard of winter snow. Both avalanches, and envelopment by blizzards undoubtedly trap and kill a number of deer in bad winter weather, just as they do sheep.

It is possible to check whether deer have actually died of starvation, by examining the upper leg bones. This can been done even with an old carcass and it does not need to be fresh. When an animal is in good condition and fat this is reflected in the white of the bone marrow. As it loses condition the marrow turns yellow, and as the animal starves and all its reserves have drained away the marrow gradually turns red. Even in old dehydrated bones the shreds of redness may be seen as evidence. In fact it takes a long time for deer to starve to death, as proved by experiments carried out in America years ago, and well over a month of starvation may be needed to kill a deer initially in good condition. It is quite a different matter with a beast in poor condition, and researchers found that 30% weight loss was a critical point. Below this recovery was problematical and doubtful. This is why run stags after the rut can be in danger in winter if they are unable to recover sufficient body condition before hard weather and resultant difficulty in obtaining adequate food supply.

It used to be thought that red deer are very healthy animals, based upon the lack of knowledge of disease in the wild herds; but when deer farming started it was soon discovered that they succumb to many diseases, and this is accentuated by keeping the beasts in a large group and restricting natural wandering over a large range. In "Some Account of Jura Red Deer" Henry Evans wrote "We seldom find dead deer quite fresh enough to open and examine them". He went to great lengths to find, examine and count dead deer, with his stalkers and employees instructed to search for them. He believed, almost certainly correctly, that many deer, especially in the north and west, die of lung worm, or husk, and liver fluke, amongst other parasites. Sheep and cattle suffering badly from liver fluke have the appearance of animals being starved; which in a sense they are, by the parasites depriving them of the nutritional benefits of their food ingestion. Without opening deer that are found dead and looking emaciated or in poor condition, and examining their livers, diagnosis of fluke infestation is not possible.

One of the major diseases encountered amongst farmed red deer in various parts of the world is Malignant Catarrhal Fever. The disease has been known to occur in cattle and a wide variety of antelope and buffalo, and has been recorded in several species of deer. It is known to occur widely amongst sheep, but without manifestation of symptoms, and a great deal of trouble arose when farmed deer were introduced onto sheep farms in New Zealand and Australia in particular, with significant numbers of deaths arising amongst the deer. The question arises as to the degree of infection and deaths of wild deer from sheep carriers of the disease in Britain.

Without doubt deer die of mineral deficiencies too. In spring cattle, and sheep, are susceptible to hypomagnesaemia, or magnesium deficiency, as a result of eating rapidly growing lush green spring grass that is low in minerals. Spring is often a time of noticeable deaths amongst wild deer, and it is probable that such a cause is equally responsible for these too. Henry Evans knew that finding deer carcasses was difficult and only a small proportion were ever discovered. He commented that this was especially so with red deer calves. These could so easily fall into peat hags or burns and disappear, as well as inevitably being eaten and the remains spread widely, if not completely removed, by scavenging carrion eaters, of which many exist in these areas.

Bearing in mind the large numbers of young red deer calves that die each season, and that comparatively few wild adult deer live beyond the age of perhaps 12 years, these numbers of deaths, over and above those shot, represent a substantial quantity of animals that die annually: yet comparatively few of these are ever found, let alone in a condition in which a post mortem examination might reveal information as to the real cause of death and the condition of the animal prior to this. Unlike sheep, deer usually retain their teeth well, and Henry Evans recorded a known hind on Jura believed to be 26 years old when she died, having produced calves regularly each year until her last, which had a complete set of teeth still at her death. Some reports suggest that stags may retain teeth less well than hinds. If this is the case it probably reflects a diet of coarser feed that was harder on their teeth.

Breeding of Red Deer

A certain amount of information about the breeding cycle of red deer has been known for many centuries, although some stalkers still seem to fail to understand the actual situation. This may arise from their failure to grasp the fact that unlike cattle that can breed all year round, since both males and females are capable of reproduction throughout the year, deer are like sheep and specifically seasonal breeders; which applies to both males and females separately. That is to say that the males come into breeding condition just as the females do. The difference is that the males, in this case red deer stags, come into season some time before the hinds do so, and remain capable of breeding for some months continuously, whereas hinds have an oestrus cycle of about eighteen to twenty-one days and can conceive only during the appropriately critical period of this, which may last little more than a few hours.

Aristotle, in ancient Greece, had worked out that the calf of a red deer was carried in the womb about eight months. He had the idea that the gestation period is based upon the potential longevity of the animal, and from this reckoned that the maximum life of a deer is thirty years. In fact his idea was basically a sound one, since both the length of the gestation period and its longevity are probably proportional to the size of the animal, and his figures were reasonably accurate. We now know that the gestation period of a red deer is about 232-235 days, with a possible idiosyncratic variation of perhaps four or five days and a bias to larger male calves being a couple of days longer than that of a smaller hind calf. Also it might be said that thirty years could be the potential maximum age of a deer, though very few in captivity and well looked after, let alone in the wild, probably actually reach the age of twenty.

Throughout the centuries the seasonal breeding period of deer has been respected, and the draconian Forest Laws that protected hunting forests from the time of William the Conqueror onwards for centuries, specified a *Time of Fence* from June 9th to July 9th when people and domestic stock were not allowed to go into the forests, in case they disturbed the deer that would be calving then. In old manuscripts the *Time of Fence* was known as *Fonneson*, which was probably derived from ancient Norman French. A second close season when deer were protected was the *Formeisun* (probably derived from the French word *fermeson* – from the French verb fermer, meaning to close). This started in October to cover the mating period.

In 1895 the Rev. H. A. Macpherson wrote, in his book on *The Red Deer* in the Fur, Feather and Fin series, "In Martindale the hinds are accustomed to take the stag from about October 20th to the beginning of December. Bell says that the red deer hind goes with young eight months and a few days. Jackson (the stalker) has told me, on different occasions, that seven months is the period of gestation, but he is no doubt mistaken in this." In fact the true gestation figure lies between these, of course, but the observation that conception does not commence until about October 20th is largely correct, as shown by comprehensive work done on Rhum by the late Brian Mitchell and others. A few precocious hinds may commence ovulation a little earlier, but the majority of red deer hinds conceive in the three weeks following October 20th. Studies carried out on deer species throughout the world to discover the synchrony of conception show that in most deer species a substantial proportion conceive within a short period of about three weeks. In Moose about 85% are reckoned to conceive within a ten day period. A study with Fallow deer suggested that 83% conceived within an eighteen day period. White-tailed deer does showed a 90% conception rate within 19 days, and two studies of Mule deer twenty years apart gave figures of 69% and 95% within a 21 day period. Reindeer have even tighter synchrony with 80% conceiving within 11 days of each other. Research into red deer suggested that 75% of hinds conceived within a fifteen day period.

This synchrony of conception is mirrored in the subsequent calving period. Dr. Charles Collyns, who wrote his classic book *The Chase of the Wild Red Deer* in 1862, about stag hunting in the West Country, held the view that "of all the animals with which I am acquainted, the hind is the most regular as regards the period of gestation. In my long experience I have known but two instances in which the hind did not drop her calf between 7th and 21st June." Late births may decrease the chance of calf survival, and one estimate suggests that the chance of calf mortality, and of lower hind fertility during the ensuing season, increases by 1% for each day of delay in giving birth beyond the normal dates.

The interesting corollary of this data, of course, is that red deer stags that come into season and rut early, and lose condition before the hinds start to come into oestrus, are unlikely to breed successfully, as already pointed out, since they will be ostracised by fitter stags. This may well apply to some big stags; and the idea that these early rutting beasts are not actually contributing to breeding, however good they are, may not fit in well with a professional stalker's management ideas!

The chart showing average red deer foetus length during the gestation period provides a guide as to the date of conception as a result of foetus measurement, which can easily be carried out during culling towards the end of the hind season when these are more readily visible.

Length of foetus in mm.

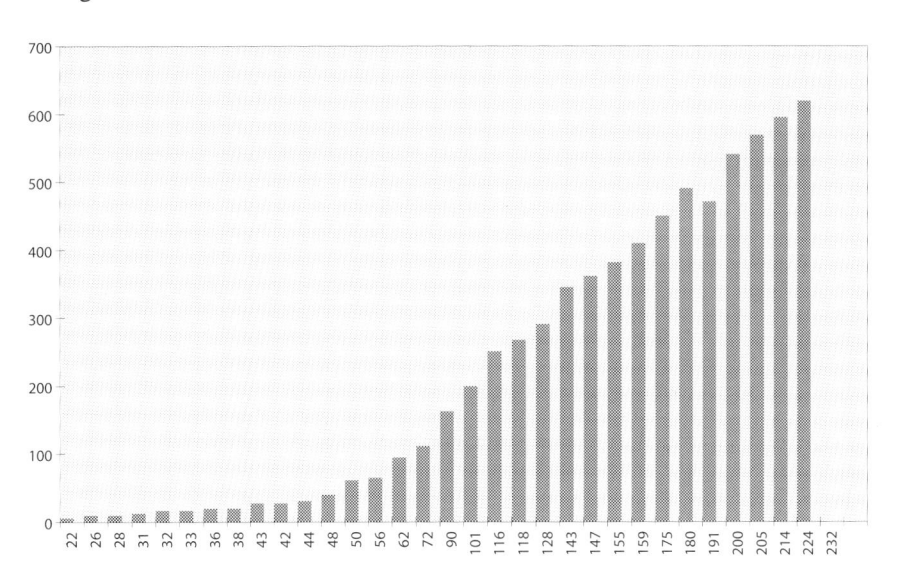

Age in Days

Most life on earth is controlled by sun light in one way or another, and deer are no exception to this. Photoperiod, or day length, controls many of their functions, of which the breeding cycle is one. This is brought about by the pineal gland in the brain reacting to darkness and secreting melatonin, which in turn causes the secretion of other hormones, and these generate various body functions. It is the change in melatonin levels that is the catalyst for these functions. Shortening days and increasing nights raise melatonin secretion duration, and this triggers the start of sexual activity in both stag and hind. This has all been proved by research, where melatonin has been administered to both stags and hinds and the result has been the advancement of seasonal behaviour. Administration of melatonin has caused a red deer stag to shed velvet in mid July and to start rutting behaviour and roaring in July/August – other stags in the group took no notice of this behaviour. Melatonin given to hinds caused these to come into oestrus early, and continuation of the administration resulted in prolonged ovarian cyclicity irrespective of the time of year.

Thus it appears that some time after the summer solstice, or the longest day, the lengthening darkness hours trigger off the hormonal activities that set in motion the breeding season. In good conditions, of ideal habitat, yearling hinds can reach puberty and come into oestrus and conceive. In some woodland areas with plenty of good feed and limited disturbance the majority of yearling red deer hinds may become pregnant, but in poorer areas of northern and western Scotland hinds may not conceive until three years old. Moreover, in good habitat most hinds will calve annually, but those in poorer condition in less hospitable environment frequently find the burden of lactation too great to achieve appropriate condition for conception and are yeld for a year as a result of failure to conceive. There is a record of a 7 month old fallow doe, age confirmed by tooth examination, which was found to be carrying a foetus.

It is rare for a red deer hind to bear twin calves, but by no means unknown. It is possible that the same situation that applies to cattle giving birth to twins also applies to red deer, whereby if the offspring are of ostensibly the opposite sex the female will be unable to breed, being a freemartin, which carries internal male organs but externally female ones. A hind in a New Zealand experiment was found to be a freemartin and records showed that she was a twin to a stag calf.

Lactation, the ability to provide the young calf with sufficient milk, is the most significant factor governing the well-being of a deer population. Without the ability to produce adequate milk for her calf the hind is unable to rear it and sustain or increase the herd. The importance of this factor cannot be over-emphasised. It may be that a number of calf deaths in the early months are due, directly or indirectly, to insufficient milk, due to poor condition of the hind, mastitis, or various other possible reasons. As already explained, failure to thrive may lead to the hummel state in young stag calves. Lactation is also a consideration in the choice of hinds for culling, for although some calves may be strong enough for precipitate weaning in winter from losing their dam, it should be borne in mind that some red deer hinds continue suckling their calves for long after the hind culling season. It is widely recorded that many hinds continue lactating well into winter, and some even until close to the birth of their next calf. A number of observations record hinds suckling yearling calves, even those with antlers. In the early 1950's several hundred red deer were shot in a nature reserve in the Crimea and records were made showing the proportion that were still lactating at different times of the year. From July – September the figure was 74%, October – December 69%, January – February 41% and March – May 32%.

Red deer milk is rich, as might be expected from the comparatively small quantity produced from her quite small udder for an animal of that size, for instance compared to domestic sheep. The calf suckles frequently in its early weeks, but less so as it gets older, and latterly may suckle only twice a day, or even once a day before weaning. As well as the importance of this high quality nourishment for the calf the bonding effect between hind and calf is also of great importance in survival.

Various data suggest that the fat content of red deer milk varies between 6.6% and 17.4%, doubtless differing between animals, and depending upon the stage during lactation. However the following table of composition gives a guide for comparison of the milk of several species:–

Milk

	Fat	crude protein	lactose
red deer	8-10%	7-9%	4-5%
cow	3.75%	3.4%	4.75%
mare	1.2%	2.0%	5.8%
ewe	6.5%	5.8%	4.8%
human	3.8%	2.1%	6.3%

The young calf will start to nibble at herbage within a few days, but will not eat a significant contribution to its food supply for several weeks. The popular notion is that the mother carefully hides the new calf in a clump of rushes or long heather, telling it to remain there until she returns. In fact the initiative is taken by the calf. After suckling it wanders off spontaneously and instinctively chooses a suitable hiding place in which to lie, observed by its mother, who remembers the location. This is the logical situation, of course, since it is necessary to obviate any scent from the mother leading a would-be predator to the site of the hidden calf. When the mother returns and requires to suckle the calf she stands a little way off and calls her offspring; which emerges from its hiding place and comes to her.

Much the same theory applies to the idea of the consumption of the afterbirth. Deer, like sheep and cattle, generally eat the afterbirth soon after parturition. Some people suggest that this is a protective action to avoid this being found by a predator and revealing the presence of the new calf. However undoubtedly the amniotic fluid and other debris leaves sufficient scent to reveal the event, and the safety procedure is to lead the calf away from the site as soon as possible. The eating of the afterbirth is an instinctive reaction probably part of that of immediately licking off the membrane surrounding the calf, particularly around its head, mouth and nostrils, and licking the calf dry. As with most wild animals in fit condition, parturition is quite rapid and comparatively easy. When she feels that birth is imminent the hind moves away from the herd or group to a place that she may consider to be more secure or private. She may not rejoin the herd or her companions with the calf for several days or even up to three weeks after the birth, until the young animal is fully active and able to keep up and interact with the others.

Hind Range

To some extent deer may be regarded as creatures of habit. Red deer hinds become hefted to an area or range, usually influenced by where they were born. However they are not territorial, and different groups of deer may use the same ground, and sometimes even join up with other groups. The size of their range obviously depends upon their habitat and weather conditions. On the open hill, for instance, the range may include different sides of a hill or glen in order to provide shelter from varying wind directions. Food availability and shelter will also influence their movements, and so their daily behaviour will vary according to food and weather and disturbance. Although red deer tend towards being crepuscular and nocturnal, they do feed in daytime too, and they have a rhythm of feeding, ruminating and resting alternately.

In summer the lactating hind has a need for a large intake of good quality feed to support her ability to produce milk, particularly in early stages when the milk demand and supply is highest. At the same time she must try to maintain or improve her own body condition to prepare for the winter, when food quality deteriorates and adverse weather makes greater demands upon her energy. Presumably as a method of helping to save energy requirements, red deer have a period in late winter when their appetite declines. This applies to captive deer offered ad lib. feed as well as to the wild ones. Whilst this means less food intake, it also means less requirement to move around using up energy at a time when food quality is at its lowest. As indicated, the stag has a period of depressed appetite at the time of the rut, and both sexes have lowered appetites in late winter, about February and March, which is a time of year when often the weather is at its worst. After this period the appetite returns, and the growth of enlarging foeti will encourage this.

Female offspring tend to remain with the maternal group, and a party of hinds will often contain several generations of the same female line. Yearling stags generally stay with the group too, but during the rut these may get chased off to the fringes by whichever rutting stag has taken over the group. During their second year they start to grow antlers, usually spikes, and in their second autumn they start to develop a noticeable mane and their testicles descend and enlarge, though remaining small until the following season. These young staggies, chased off by rutting adult stags tend to form small groups. Their departure from their dams is not entirely due to being chased off by older stags however, since the young stags, much like teenage humans with growing testosterone levels, spontaneously choose to wander from their home territory. Undoubtedly the initiative to leave their dam is taken by the yearling stag in many instances.

Whilst the change from summer to winter coat is more obvious with a stag, that of the hind is more imperceptible. From August onwards the stag's hair begins to darken and his mane grows, until by mid September he appears to be in full winter coat, generally making himself appear substantially darker as a result of wallowing in mud. The hind's change to winter coat is more gradual. The growth of grey winter hair is more obvious on her legs. The summer hair is not shed, as most literature suggests, but the red hairs grow longer and thicker and hollow, to give more insulation. Whilst through the summer coat grows a thicker winter coat of long hollow grey hairs. Where summer coat may have been rubbed off, subsequently being replaced by the winter coat, the pelage is grey, but where the red tipped summer hairs are retained the coat is noticeably flecked with red and still appears red, albeit darker, in some light.

Later in the season a layer of under-wool grows on the neck and back, as added insulation. This wool layer growth may be affected to some degree by temperature, since it appears to be more obvious, in greater quantity, at shedding time after a harder winter.

The colour of the pelage of red deer varies quite a lot, not only with the positioning and extent of the white or buff, and black markings on the rump, but also the overall pelage colour. At a distance the coat colour can appear to change according to whether dry or wet, or in different lights, but close examination will reveal different shades of coat, particularly in winter. Alexander Macrae, in his *Handbook of Deer-*

stalking published in 1880, wrote "Some of them are yellow, called golden colour; others are somewhat brownish; and the third are somewhat of a dark blue. The first two kinds have the best haunches; the other kind may be in fair condition, and well tasted, but they seldom have fat haunches. There are occasional light-grey ones, apparently old hinds, that are in good condition.". The degree of veracity in this observation may be open to doubt. Nevertheless the keen observer can notice occasional small idiosyncratic variations in colour markings between red deer that may enable distinction between animals of similar size and shape.

Much of the communication between deer would seem to be visual, but there is a degree of vocal contact too. Hinds call to their offspring, and the calves call to their dams. Because their auditory senses are so well developed it is probable that some of the sounds are not readily audible to the human ear, particularly at a distance, but it seems likely that these sounds, in the form of bleats and squeaks, carry further and are more easily heard by other deer than most humans can appreciate. There is no doubt about the alarm signal of a disturbed hind, though. Even on the open hill, but much more so in woodland, the resonant alarm bark is loud and unmistakeable and can be heard over a considerable distance. A hind that is alarmed will flare her nostrils, with ears pricked, and if her reaction is hostile rather than fearful, by the presence of a dog or fox near her calf for instance, she will flare up the hair on her caudal area and raise the hairs of her mane and a strip all down the centre of her back. She may also trot a few steps in what has been described as a stotting or pronking mode.

Red deer groups have a definite hierarchy or pecking order, and this can be observed when watching hinds feeding, and groups of stags in velvet too. Hinds can be aggressive and strike a severe blow with their front feet and sharp hooves. They can raise their forefeet quite high for this purpose, and generally such a kick is sufficient to establish, or re-establish, authority in the group. Sometimes fighting involves standing up on their hind legs and boxing with both fore feet. This action is often seen amongst young stags in velvet. Red deer are able to balance well when standing vertically on their hind feet, as demonstrated if one watches these feeding on the leaves of trees, when they can stand up on their hind legs to reach higher leaves for a minute at least at a time.

An integral part of all deerstalking is the search and constant observation for signs of deer. On open ground the emphasis may seem to be upon scanning the countryside with binoculars or telescope looking for deer, but it is still important to look for deer sign on the ground too, in order to build up a picture of deer presence and behaviour. In woodland, of course, this is even more important, since the chances are substantially greater that the deer will see the unwary stalker first. On damp ground tracks are often obvious, but on dry ground these are much less so. Signs of feeding may be difficult to detect since deer are very delicate feeders, capable of nipping off buds and shoots from quite small twigs without leaving much evidence. Flattened grass where deer have been lying is another sign of both their presence and activity. Droppings are probably the most obvious sign of the previous presence of deer

In their search for some method of establishing an acceptable estimate of deer populations in woodland, or for numbers of deer utilising certain areas of open ground, some scientific researchers have adopted the counting of droppings, or piles of droppings, as a method of extrapolating deer numbers, based upon the premise that the average deer defaecates 13 times a day. The establishment of the population of deer in a given range of open country is difficult, even when teams of people with some experience endeavour to walk the ground and count deer seen. Weather conditions can influence the degree of deer presence at any particular time, and even repeated counts under a variety of conditions might produce varied results, quite apart from the influence of the disturbance caused by the counts themselves. In woodland the task is daunting. Repeated experiments in Denmark, with red, fallow and roe deer, on carefully studied small areas, such as islands or enclosed woodland, have revealed the enormous difficulty in judging numbers, which are invariably underestimated. Careful observation of deer feeding and resting and moving about, over a period, suggests that the counting of droppings is a rather forlorn desperate attempt at achieving data that is no substitute for many hours of careful observation and study. Those that have so observed red deer in this way and then examined the area for signs will be all too aware of this situation. Deer, as with many animals, tend to defaecate after their period of resting; this following a period of feeding and then another of ruminating and consuming the food gathered. They also often do so when disturbed, or when slightly excited, such as when crossing a river or other obstacle for instance. The same behaviour is seen when moving sheep and cattle, and they too exhibit the same trait for voiding their waste products after resting to digest their food. This does not mean to say that deer do not defaecate at other times of course, and they certainly do so when feeding and moving too, but it does indicate the emphasis upon the variation in this activity that suggests great caution in attempting to use such a measure to extrapolate numbers present.

Judging Age

The judgement of the age of red deer tends not to be a matter of science or art but a combination of both. Undoubtedly the ability to watch the animal alive, followed by examination of the carcass, gives the best opportunity for correct age assessment. Describing the looks of an animal in written terms is difficult, and there is little satisfactory substitute for experience. Red deer stags tend to develop improved antler growth during their early years, until maturity, and the pedicles tend to thicken with each seasonal re-growth of antler. However, since antler growth is influenced by feeding to a significant degree, disruption to this, for instance by a decline in health, may well upset this sequence. Moreover a young stag of say four years old in fine woodland habitat may develop antlers as large as, or better than, an eight year old stag living on open hill ground not far away, and travelling to seek hinds in the rut could easily lead to one moving temporarily to different ground. So antlers alone may not be any guide to age.

Size, too, is influenced by food, but generally larger thicker set animals are older in a given habitat. More reliable in age judgement is a difficult to define look of the face, and the shape and movement of the animal, the interpretation of which relies upon experience, rather in the same way that humans are able to a degree to instinctively judge the approximate age group of fellow humans as a result of noting a variety of different aspects.

Hinds, with no antlers, and more similar body shapes and sizes, present a more difficult ageing problem. Some old hinds seem obvious as a result of poor condition due to age, but this may be accentuated by comparison with her companions. Milk hinds inevitably look rather thinner and more angular, with possibly less glossy coats, than yeld hinds; for the obvious reason that a significant part of their food intake is utilised for milk production rather than building up body condition and fat reserves. One guide to the age of a hind is the length of her face and its more angular appearance. If one studies a group of hinds resting, so that comparison of their head shape is easier, it can often be seen that some older hinds have very long faces, almost to becoming comparatively caricatural.

Age judgement of a dead deer is usually confirmed by examination of the teeth. In the first few years of the animal's life tooth growth is progressive and an accurate guide to age, but thereafter the assessment becomes rather subjective. There is a view that sectioning teeth gives scientific evidence of age, since these develop growth rings with some similarity to those found in trees, denoting seasonal growth. However some tests have suggested that this evidence is not conclusive. When this idea was first promoted, the National Veterinary Laboratory in Stockholm carried out an experiment to test the efficacy of tooth sectioning as a guide to age in roe deer, and as a result decided that the original assessment by tooth wear was more reliable.

Undoubtedly the diet of the deer will affect tooth wear, as health will affect tooth retention. Some deer have strange eating habits, and one imagines that those attracted to chewing antlers and bones will show greater tooth wear than others. Cast antlers invariably eventually are chewed and gnawed completely. Whilst small rodents such as voles and mice may gnaw these, particularly in woodland, the deer certainly do so quite deliberately. Indeed deer will chew all sorts of bones. Several cases have been reported of deer with bones stuck in their mouths, particularly pelvic bones of sheep or deer, where the foramen, or hole, in these is of a size to fit the lower jaw of a deer.

Henry Evans reported that deer not only ate the bones but the skin of carcasses as well and wrote that he had found deer consuming the remains whilst still decomposing and stinking. Another report told of an old horse being shot and left to lie out on the hill in spring. In August hinds were seen to come and eat the bones and by November there was nothing left.

This habit is often attributed to a requirement of the deer for minerals, but it is difficult to differentiate between needing and liking, and between requirement and taste. It may surprise people to know that deer have strange eating habits on occasion, including carnivorous ones. There have been a number of reports of red deer being observed eating frogs, birds' eggs, fish, feathers, and even a dead sparrow, so it will be no surprise, therefore, to learn that on deer farms the deer are commonly seen eating their cast antler buttons (the coronets remaining after the farmed deer have had their antlers cut off) and shed velvet. Caribou are reported as deliberately raiding nests of eider ducks and geese on the tundra to eat eggs, and cattle have also been observed eating both fish on beaches and bones and dead rabbits. It is likely that much of this behaviour revolves around individual tastes of deer, just as occurs with humans. This is easily seen amongst hand fed captive deer, where some like to eat banana or avocado skins, or orange peel, where others reject these. Peppermints and chocolate biscuits are favourite treats for some captive deer, and these can scent barley grains hidden in long grass. Some will eat types of fungi that others ignore, and at different seasons different leaves seem to have more attraction. Amongst the stranger Cervid eating habits was a report of a taste for cigarettes by both captive red and roe deer, and most particularly the account of a red deer hind at a New Zealand research station who appeared to like cigarette (but not pipe) smoke, and would actually suck this in and blow it out through her nostrils!

Red deer are browsers, not grazers, as is indicated by the shape of their mouths, not having wide grazing muzzles like cattle, but the more delicate narrower shape of eclectic feeders. As well as grass and forbs and heather eaten on the open hill, given the opportunity red deer will eat hawthorn, rowan, ash, gean, beech and oak buds and leaves, and silver birch at times, as well as willow, and even holly in winter, amongst others. They will seek out bramble leaves in woodland, and ivy, and fruits such as broom pods and acorns. They particularly favour lichens growing upon trees or old timber.

Logically it would seem unlikely that the penchant for the chewing of antlers and bones by deer derived purely from a craving for calcium or other minerals generated by a deficiency, since such a deficiency would manifest itself in other ways and lead to a noticeable decrease in the well-being of the animals. The idea that the deer just like the smell or taste of these things, coupled with curiosity, seems more likely, and the habit appears to be more akin to dogs or young cattle chewing, and sometimes ingesting, strange objects.

In judging the age of deer by tooth wear allowance must be made for such habits, and the general feeding circumstances of the animals.

TWO YEAR OLD STAG

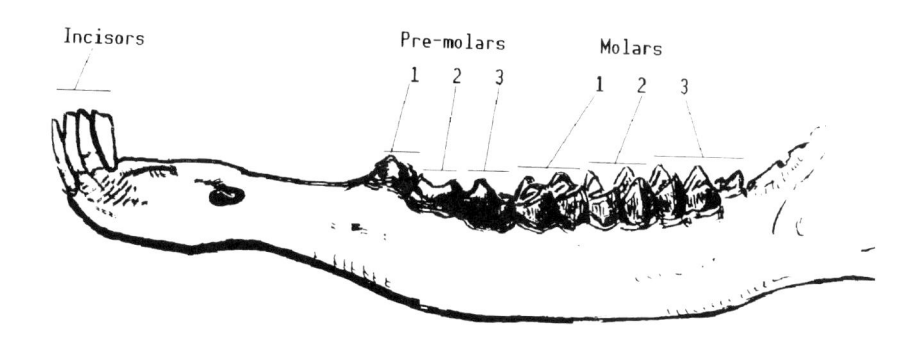

The determination of the age of farm livestock by tooth examination has been in use for centuries, particularly in younger animals. The old saying that one should not look a gift horse in the mouth originates from this; it means that one should not check to see that it is a young animal. Sheep are the livestock most checked in this way to decide age, but these are judged by their incisor teeth, which have a definite and slow pattern of emergence. Teeth are of vital importance in sheep husbandry, and it is traditional to sell off from the hard heather hills those ewes that are either losing their incisor teeth or about to do so, because without these in good order their ability to eat sufficiently well to maintain condition is impaired. The incisors of sheep, the front cutting teeth, start to change from small milk teeth to larger permanent ones at between a year and fifteen months old when the central pair are replaced by noticeably bigger ones. The remaining three pairs are steadily replaced at six month intervals or longer thereafter until the animal has what is known as a full mouth.

In the case of red deer the replacement of milk or calf incisor teeth by permanent ones is far more rapid and this is completed by the time that the animal is a two year old. Therefore the incisor teeth only offer a guide for differentiating between a calf, which has four pairs of milk front teeth, and a yearling where the central two pairs have been replaced by much larger permanent ones, and finally a two year old where all the incisor teeth are permanent ones. Thereafter it is necessary to examine the back teeth to decide age.

In an adult animal there are six back grinding teeth on each jawbone, the front three of which, at first glance perhaps appearing a little more rounded in a younger deer, are called pre-molars, and the back three are molars. The hindmost of the latter has three cusps, whereas the others have two only. These pre-molars and molars develop in the growing young deer both in type and number. A calf has three milk pre-molars and as yet only one molar. This is destined to be a permanent tooth but it has hollow open-ended roots, which can be seen if the tooth is extracted from the jawbone. The three smaller milk pre-molars remain as a yearling but a second molar appears. The root ends of the first molar have closed up by then but those of the new second one remain open. In a two year old red deer, which is to say one in its third season, or carrying its second set of antlers in the case of a stag, (the calf having been born in June) the milk pre-molars are replaced by permanent ones (which at that stage may be found to be rather loose in a cleaned jawbone). The third molar also appears, and this has open fragile roots, whilst those of the second have closed up. This third, back, molar has three cusps, of which the hindmost one is small initially. This last cusp is definitive between a two year old and a three year old because in the case of the former it is white and unstained. By the time that the animal is a three year old this becomes stained and more worn.

Extensive research into the dentition of red deer, using beasts of known age, including tagged animals and park deer, suggested no discernible difference in tooth wear between stags and hinds of similar ages. It also suggested little difference in wear between deer from different areas. However it is likely that there may be difference in practice dependent upon the type of food eaten and upon idiosyncratic performance, as there is in all animals. The same will apply to the degree of any tooth loss in old deer.

Once the animal has a full mouth age assessment is no longer precise but a matter of judgement and comparison. From about five years onwards tooth wear begins to be noticeable and by the time that the animal is ten years old considerable wear of the back teeth is likely. In older animals the wear may be excessive and there may even be tooth loss. However it is extremely rash to be pedantic in views about this. Some old deer that have had access to good food and maintained excellent condition can retain all their teeth to great age, and it is as well to recall that Henry Evans recorded a hind judged to be at least 26 years old that was found to have retained all her teeth when discovered dead. After all one only has to consider the differences in human teeth, where some people have considerable dental problems yet others have none and retain their own until a great age.

Judgement of the back teeth of deer is impossible without a degree of surgery on the head of the beast, and really is satisfactory only with the jawbone removed and cleaned so that it can be examined properly. Some stalkers carry out this procedure meticulously and retain the jaws with the heads in an attempt to learn about the selection and management policies over the years. This is mostly done with stags, and substantially less identification is carried out with hinds, to which very little attention is generally paid in comparison to stags.

The best assessment of the age of deer is by a combination of the impression formed from observation of the live animal, the overall appearance of the carcase, in the case of a stag the thickness of the pedicles, and by judgement of the growth and wear of the teeth.

The Development of Woodland Stalking

At the present time woodland deer stalking may refer to the pursuit of fallow deer, Japanese sika, Muntjac, or roe deer. The former two species are localised, and though muntjac are spreading rapidly in southern England, their situation and their habit of breeding without definite seasons, make them a rather more specialised type of stalking. In this treatise woodland stalking is taken to refer in detail only to the now almost ubiquitous roe deer, although many of the aspects refer to the stalking of any type of deer, including woodland red deer, the pursuit of which is quite different from stalking on the open hill.

Half a century ago Britain was recovering from several long years of costly war. Rebuilding and new buildings required vast quantities of timber, and landowners were encouraged to plant trees and replant the many woods that had been felled to contribute to the war effort. This meant that effectively since the middle of the century there has been continuous tree planting, led by the Forestry Commission. In 1953 the rabbit disease myxomatosis, introduced to this country from France, hit the British rabbit population and by 1955 had wiped out an estimated 99% of the rabbits in Britain. This had two results that affected and assisted the increase in the roe population. Firstly, with rabbits virtually non-existent in most areas fencing against these was no longer so important, and with few deer there was no point in the expense of fencing against these; so access to young plantations was easy for roe. Secondly, with no rabbits to consume this, the undergrowth flourished, providing rich feeding habitat for the deer.

With cover from the growing plantations of trees and abundant food within these during the early years of the tree growth, the ideal habitat resulted in a substantial upsurge in the population of not only roe deer, but of other species too. By the late 1960's the roe and fallow deer populations in areas such as Sussex, Surrey, and Dorset and others, had expanded to high levels and the animals began to be regarded as a nuisance to both farm crops and gardens, as well as to forestry. At that time woodland stalking was an interest of only a handful of enthusiasts, and deer were culled, particularly in forestry areas, by shotgun drives and snaring, both cruel methods that soon became to be regarded as unacceptably inhumane. The increased deer problems led to the formation of a local deer control society by one resourceful farmer. This idea quickly spread and deer control societies sprang up in a number of places in southern Britain, and were encouraged by the British Deer Society as a humane method of having the deer controlled by being shot by rifles in experienced hands.

Within a few years the number of would-be woodland deerstalkers grew, as the deer population continued to spread, and continental stalkers became increasingly aware of the availability and quality of British deer and discovered that obtaining stalking in this country was easier than in their own. With this growing competition for stalking the landowners and foresters began to realise that the deer were not simply pests but a valuable sporting asset, and that they could have the deer controlled and achieve an income from them at the same time. Nowadays the emphasis has changed from controlling the deer to what is described as managing them, both for keeping numbers under control and ensuring best returns from the sporting asset.

Roe Deer

The roe is the most widespread species of deer in Britain as well as the most numerous, and it has consistently increased both its population and range over the past several decades, taking advantage of the ideal habitat provided by new forests and farm woodlands. One estimate suggests that there are between 300,000 and 600,000 roe deer in Britain, but the disparity in the extremes of these figures indicates the impossibility of trying to guess numbers of such an elusive woodland animal. Even the top figure might be a gross under-estimate. Roe occur widely throughout the whole of Scotland and northern England, and in large numbers in southern counties, with isolated populations in East Anglia, but in recent years they have spread more into midland counties. They cause damage in young forestry plantations and to any newly planted tree saplings, resulting in significant extra expense for protection, and can be a nuisance in suburban and country gardens eating plants and shrubs, but nevertheless they are delightful graceful little animals that can also give pleasure to many people.

The majority of people used to seeing roe deer, including stalkers, are quite unaware of the actual size of these animals, or indeed of any deer. As shown in the diagram earlier the height of a live roe at the shoulder is only just over two feet. That is to say the deer only comes up to around the knee of a tall man and is about the same size as a large Labrador dog. At a live weight of between 50 and 60lbs on average, their weight may be less than a stockier built dog, although the weights of roe do vary considerably in differing habitats, and those in less hospitable parts of northern Scotland may weigh substantially less than animals from Surrey or Sussex for instance.

The lifestyle and life cycle of roe differs completely from that of red deer. The roe is a solitary creature and not a herd animal, though in winter family parties group together, and in some very open parts of Europe so-called 'Field roe' can be found in parties of over twenty animals or more in winter, lying out in the middle of large fields. Such large groups are rarely seen in Britain, and parties of numbers into double figures are unusual. In winter the roe tend to have a range in which they live, but in summer they become more territorial and frequent a much smaller area and are often protective of this as regards other roe deer of the same sex. This territory is based upon the doe and her chosen area for having and raising her kids.

A popular theory is that roe bucks are territorial, and that in summer these establish well defined territories that they guard from other bucks, marking the area out with fraying and scraping and leaving their scent, and regularly patrolling the boundaries of their chosen patch. Undoubtedly the habitat plays a significant role in the behaviour of the bucks; but the interpretation of their behaviour into the concept that a master buck rules an area and will keep out other intruders, and so therefore the stalker should leave such master bucks unharmed to ensure that they keep other bucks away, requires much thought. Bucks tend to have a range rather than a specific territory, and this may encompass or encroach upon the smaller territories of several does. Much of the apparent territory marking, by fraying trees, takes place in spring. Initially this may be to assist cleaning the drying velvet skin from their newly hardened antlers; but in understanding the biology of the roe it becomes apparent that the behaviour is hormonally influenced. The violent fraying of trees is a manifestation of the rise in testosterone, which is responsible for the hardening and cleaning of the antlers, and the behaviour is similar to that of red deer stags at the start of the rut, when full of testosterone and the aggression that accompanies the frustration of no females in season they vent their feelings on saplings and on any other males that they meet. Some authorities suggest that this apparent territorial marking is not defensive or aggressive, and probably done for the buck's own benefit, since the reaction, if any, of other deer encountering such marking does not suggest that it conveys any warning signal.

This flush of hormonal activity in spring can lead to almost a false rut situation on occasion, with bucks chasing does, or shadowing them for a long time, their behaviour governed by androgen influenced instinct.

Some theorists devise a management plan for culling roe bucks in summer based upon this supposed master buck theory, or upon the idea that medal quality antlers are entirely genetic. However, generalisation is not advisable, because circumstances and habitats differ widely. Objectives differ too. If venison is a consideration, from the point of view of quality or value, for instance, then there is little point in starting stalking too early in the season in many northern areas where the roe condition will have deteriorated over winter and many yearlings can produce carcasses of only 25lbs or less. It may be wiser to wait until early summer when they have grown to better condition. On the other hand, if the concern is mainly about deer numbers, then an early start on yearlings may be advisable, since these are often more obvious in spring, hungrily emerging to feed on lush new growth on the field edges, as their seasonal appetite reduction recedes and is replaced by the incentive to feed upon the fresh new plants.

In spring there is a general movement of roe deer, partly due to animals emerging from their winter habitat to their chosen summer areas, and partly due to young animals emigrating to find new places in which to spend the summer. It is often suggested that this emigration of yearling roe is caused by the doe chasing her offspring away. This may be so, since roe are solitary animals in summer, clearly disliking the presence of other roe in their immediate vicinity – except occasionally poorly developed yearling bucks that sometimes associate with each other for the early part of the summer – and particularly the pregnant does that choose a patch in which to have and raise their kids. On the other hand it is very likely that it is actually the yearlings that take the initiative to wander off, as do many young mammals at a similar stage of puberty, including humans. It may not be possible to identify whether a yearling seen chased is actually the offspring of the chaser or a stranger wandering through. Some of the chasing seen is clearly more in the nature of play than aggression.

At this time of year, in early spring, when some deer have not clearly decided where to stay for the summer, the stalker might well take advantage of the opportunity of maximising the buck cull, if it is a requirement to achieve a high cull number in an area thought to be heavily populated by the deer. It is quite possible that a number of bucks seen early in the season are itinerary rather than residential and will not be seen again on the ground. Indeed in areas of thick cover and plentiful food for the roe it may well be that many of the bucks, even residents, seen during the early part of the season are not seen again, so that advantage should be taken of opportunities that arise as they do so.

Roe bucks seen in late winter, with antlers in velvet, often appear to have remarkably impressive heads, but these may be difficult to identify again once the antlers have hardened and been cleaned. Not only does the velvet make the antlers appear to be much thicker than actually transpires when they are clean, but they also appear longer. The velvet is composed of skin covered by hair, and although this is of different texture to the body hair or even that on the face, being much smoother and softer, hence the description velvet, it still is hair growth. An interesting experiment with red deer that were made to grow antlers at six monthly intervals showed that the hair on the velvet of the antlers grown in winter was longer than that grown on summer antlers. Thus it may be that the hair on roe antlers, which are grown through the winter, is proportionately longer than the hair on the summer grown antlers of other species, creating an illusion of bigger growth as a result of the covering designed to give greater insulation.

There is much dogmatic lore about roe antlers, and the choice of which bucks to shoot, with a view to managing the population to improve antler growth and the trophies that the bucks provide. Most of this originated on the continent, particularly from Germany, where there is a long tradition of roe stalking. However a study of the results of the long practice of the ideals recognised there, and comparison with the state of roe deer in Britain in the last few decades, provides interesting observations. Many years of selective shooting on the continent can be seen to have produced no significant result in terms of trophy improvement in roe. In Britain, where selectivity is not so universally practised, it is evident that many high quality roe have been observed and shot, and these have been present in areas that not only have high quality feed available for the deer, but usually have been either newly colonised areas or places with a comparatively low or spread out population of deer. There is little doubt that the most important factors influencing the size of both roe body weight and antler growth are food supply, shelter and stress. The latter means not only freedom from much human disturbance, but also limited stress caused by the presence of competing deer. There are many examples of areas where roe body weight and antler quality have reduced in inverse proportion to the growth of the population of the animals in the area. Genetic traits, particularly antler shape, may have influence; but only in a secondary manner to these more important factors. Winter weather, during the period when roe antlers are growing, undoubtedly has some effect upon seasonal antler growth, in that food may be scarcer or poorer quality and the buck's ability to forage for it curtailed, and their bodily condition thus less favourable.

It has been demonstrated repeatedly that assessment of the population of roe in an area is extremely difficult, and invariably underestimated. In an area where roe are of poor quality there is probably a case for attempting to reduce numbers as a step towards improving quality. Research in Denmark years ago studied four widely different areas and the roe inhabiting these. One area was good agricultural land, and another poor sandy coniferous woodland and heath habitat. The soils were analysed, as were the stomach contents of roe shot in both places, and so on. The conclusion was that the poorer area was as capable of producing high quality bucks as the richer ground, since the population in the former was lower, so that there were fewer deer to compete for what quality herbage there was to be found, and by being eclectic the feed intake of the roe on the poorer ground was as good, or better than that where more deer were competing with each other. This has been demonstrated in Britain too, where impressive antlered roe bucks have been found on high heather hills and not only in rich agricultural areas.

One aspect of roe deer management often preached, not only on the continent, but also in Britain, is the idea that roe antlers increase in quality annually, and thus so-called 'promising' two or three year old bucks are left to improve antler quality in later years. Some professional stalkers claim that by carefully adopting this policy they have improved the numbers of medal quality heads on their ground. From an aesthetic point of view it is rather invidious to criticise this approach, but in practice the reality is that roe deer antlers do not necessarily improve progressively, but reflect the conditions experienced during their period of growth. A gold medal head one summer may not be even of medal standard the following year. Similarly known yearling bucks have produced antlers of medal standard. As with red deer the pedicles, and the coronets, increase in thickness with age, but, as stated, the actual growth of the antler during the winter months is influenced by the food intake and the condition of the buck during the period.

Roe deer hummels, or bucks without antlers, are very rare. Considerably more so than with red deer. Nevertheless they do occur. When these have been reported the circumstances suggest similarity to the cause of this condition in red deer, namely poor growth in the kid, possibly due to insufficient milk supply, or illness. It is quite likely that a number of roe kids in such situations, that would have become hummels, actually die during their first winter, and so this condition is not revealed. In some areas of poorer country, mostly in the north of Britain, some yearling bucks produce only very small spikes of antlers. Sometimes these do not shed the velvet in early summer when other bucks show hardened clean antlers. Occasionally this occurs with a buck older than a yearling. The reason for this is hormonal.

The hormonal and antler cycle of roe is quite different from that of red deer and other species. In the first place the antlers are cast in early winter and re-grow through the winter, hardening and cleaning in the spring. This procedure is connected to the seasonal hormonal and breeding activity of the buck. Unlike red deer stags that have an increase in secretion of testosterone in late August or early September, causing antler ossification and cleaning and other male breeding characteristics, which lasts until perhaps December, the roe buck experiences two photoperiodically influenced testosterone increases during the year. The first occurs in Spring, which leads to antler hardening and cleaning, after which the testosterone level falls, until mid July when it rises again for the rut, and falls again in late August.

The spring testosterone rise results in the anticipated associated activities of the roe bucks. There is a noticeable increase in the interest in does, which, not being in season, are not receptive to these advances. Sometimes one can witness almost a false rut in spring as a result of this activity in a buck with high testosterone level. The hormone secretion does not fall off completely, leading to antler casting, of course, until early winter. The most obvious result of the spring rise in male hormone is the manifestation of aggression and frustration resulting in fraying of saplings and bushes, often leading to much damage in areas of newly planted trees, and also the display of aggression towards other bucks.

This hormone generated behaviour is usually anthropomorphically interpreted as territory marking and defence.

In the case of some yearlings it would seem that the spring rise of testosterone levels is either insufficient, or perhaps non-existent, probably due to low body condition, to precipitate antler hardening and cleaning, so that velvet is not shed. It is noticeable that young bucks still in velvet seem to be more playful, and to enjoy the company of their fellows in Spring, and are tolerated by older bucks, which may be a reflection of their low androgen content. Inevitably these animals do shed the velvet with the July testosterone increase, since bucks still in velvet are not seen late in the summer.

Stalking Roe

Roe deer must surely be the daintiest and most beautiful of all deer. Anyone who has had the experience of having a tame roe come to sniff one and be friendly becomes all too aware that these delicate little animals only stand at a level with about one's knee. The watcher studying the deer through binoculars and the stalker viewing them through a telescopic sight obtain an exaggerated impression of size. Because of their diminutive stature roe prefer to scramble underneath fences or through holes rather than jump these, despite adequate ability to jump. Roe can climb through a conventional five bar gate more easily than a large dog. Consequently entry into gardens is not difficult for roe deer in most situations.

    The variety of habitat occupied by roe is very wide in Britain. They are found in marshy land, open intensively farmed areas, woodland and on the open hills to over the 2,000 feet level, but more normally they are woodland creatures, being primarily eclectic browsers. Like red deer they have a period in winter when their appetite appears smaller and they move about less, and they become more nocturnal, particularly in areas affected by human disturbance. In undisturbed areas roe can often be found out feeding on fine sunny days in winter in the middle of the day. Like all ruminants they have a cycle of feeding, followed by a period of ruminating, and then one of resting. These activities are influenced by both the weather and disturbance. Deer do not like strong wind, or heavy rain, and seek shelter in these conditions.

In spring the roe are tempted out into field edges and the outside of woodland or open clearings, where the sunlight has encouraged the early growth of new spring vegetation, before growth in more sheltered places has commenced. Spring and early summer is also a time for the movement of roe to their chosen summer haunts, with the split up of the winter family groups, and with the younger animals wandering off to find summer locations of their own. This is a time of year when stalkers may see more activity of bucks and perhaps observe some animals that they may not see again later in the season. The spring hormonal flush results in bucks becoming active, as well as the urge to feed on the new year's growth and restore condition that may have been lost in winter. The does will also be subject to the increasing pressure of the food demands of their pregnancy.

Even in summer roe deer are primarily crepuscular and nocturnal, and early mornings and evenings are generally the best time to find them, although midday may be a good time in some areas too. Roe seem to look upwards less than red and fallow deer, and high seats are a very effective aid to both stalking and observing them in the evenings. Often that time in the gloaming when the woodcock emerges for his roding patrol of his territory is the time when the roe materialise out of the woodland cover into clearings. High seats are less practical for morning observation because of the difficulty in reaching these when the deer may already be out feeding. There is sense in the old German adage which says that the stalker should walk in the mornings and sit in the evenings. It has to be remembered, when walking through the woods, just how small roe deer really are, and that their line of sight is possibly around the level of human knees, and so they are able to see at a level below herbage that may obscure human view. So often the first indication of the presence of a deer to a stalker in woods is the tell-tale clicking of an animal's cleaves, or hooves, as it runs off. It is uncertain whether this noise is deliberate, as a warning signal, or occasioned by the method of movement of somewhat unhurried, but nevertheless alarmed, flight. Many hoofed animals make the sound at times, including cattle and sheep and antelopes, and both reindeer and eland are known for their hoof clicking noise as they walk. On occasions one can hear the noise made by an undisturbed roe walking past when one is concealed close to the deer in very still conditions.

Very often a roe deer, having observed a human, or some other object of unease to it, will stand still, hoping to remain unobserved; rather as a rabbit or pheasant will crouch down and hide if it believes that it has not been seen. Movement is all important in directing attention, to both deer and human, and often a roe will stand perfectly still, perhaps partly obscured by a bush, hoping to remain undetected, following the intruder only with its eyes and slow turning of its head to watch the object of its attention; a strategy that is frequently successful.

The antlers of roe bucks harden, and they clean off the newly dead velvet, in April or May, depending upon the area, and upon their age, although in the south of England in some seasons older bucks may be observed cleaning antlers as early as late February; for younger bucks clean their antlers later than older ones, since their spring testosterone flush tends to be a little later. This activity, as explained, is governed by raised testosterone levels, which in turn is influenced by photoperiod, or the decrease in melatonin secretion resulting from shorter nights and longer days in spring. Thus bucks in southern England clean their antlers earlier in the season than those in northern Scotland. The reaction to hormonal activity may be idiosyncratic to a degree, which accounts for the cleaning of some bucks before others, but age and development result in higher testosterone levels in mature animals, so that these shed their velvet earlier than yearlings.

The Spring moult and change into summer coat is rather different. It would appear that this is also hormonally influenced, and affected by photoperiod, as has been shown experimentally, but it is possible that weather conditions and temperature also play their part in instigating this mechanism. Contrary to the antler change, mature roe seem slower in completing their change to summer pelage than young deer, and in some seasons older beasts can still show some signs of remaining winter hair well into June in northern Scotland.

There is a degree of variation in the markings of roe summer coats whereby some distinction can be made between animals from careful observation. The antlers may be the obvious feature with bucks; but care must be taken to be certain that there is not more than one buck present in the vicinity with a similar head. Such has been recorded, even with unusually formed antlers thought to be easily recognised. The facial markings of bucks differ to quite a significant extent, with differing amounts of greyness and variation in the actual expression resulting from the white patches around the mouth and nose. Also, in some areas there is a substantial variation in colour of the caudal area, around the tail and backside. Many observers and stalkers unfamiliar with roe deer in other areas are unaware that these differ. Stalkers from Surrey and Sussex, for instance, have been astonished to learn that in Scotland, and parts of Dorset for instance, roe in summer coat have white caudal patches of varying size; whilst stalkers in many Scottish areas may be equally astonished to discover that in some parts of southern England the summer roe have no white on their backsides. The distribution of these white caudal patch summer markings in Britain, and indeed on the continent, is not known. In some parts of Europe the roe have no summer white backsides, and in other areas both occur. It would seem likely that the trait is hereditary. In those places where white summer caudal patches occur in the unhared coats of roe deer, the size of the white area varies quite considerably, from a small patch around or below the tail, to a large caudal disk easily seen from a sideways view. Sometimes the patch is buff or sandy coloured.

Another distinguishing feature where there is noticeable variation between individual deer is the hairiness of the insides of their ears and the colour of this. Some deer seem to have much hairier ears than others and with some the hair is noticeably whiter than the usual fawn colour. A further aspect that sometimes misleads stalkers when judging the size of the antlers of a roe buck is that the length of their ears differ. As a rough guide, some roe have ears five inches long whereas others have them up to six inches long. Needless to say, if one is judging antler length by ear length a buck whose antlers might appear to be twice the length of his ears could have a two inch variation in length, and this must be allowed for with the assessment.

Occasionally white roe have been reported from different parts of Britain, but these are very rare; and even more so are skewbald animals, with white patches on the body. In parts of Germany black roe deer occur, and in some of these places in significant numbers. These have been recorded since the sixteenth century, and there is some thought that the black roe represent a very old strain, since it is reported that the percentage of these with vestigial canine teeth occurring in the upper jaw is significantly greater than with normal red roe. It is also reported that the black roe have longer tails. The latter, tail length variations, occur very infrequently in red British roe. The tail of a roe deer is tiny, of course, and scarcely noticeable in a live animal until it raises this to defaecate. In cutting out the rectum of a deer during gralloching a stalker will notice the tiny tail, and it is worth checking to see if this might be longer than normal.

Roe deer are eclectic feeders, choosing the most nutritious herbage and food items where these are available. As well as young shoots and leaves they are very fond of flowers and buds to eat. They also like and seek out the fruits of the forest in season, such as fallen nuts and acorns, and fungi. In winter, when food is difficult to find in hard weather roe will eat the growing shoots of young conifer trees, and other plants that they might eschew in summer when the variety available is greater and more appealing. Roe will eat ragwort, and in badly infested fields where these plants have been conspicuously avoided and left by farm livestock in hard weather roe will eat them down to the roots. They will also eat root crops in winter, and in the north in hard weather roe can often be seen in turnip fields even in day time, sometimes in significant numbers where the presence of a root crop may attract deer from a large area of surrounding woodland.

It is the predilection for food of high nutritional value that cause roe deer to be a nuisance in gardens. They are fond of many flowers and flower buds, particularly roses, and often seem to concentrate upon especially prized plants in the garden. The deer also have a particular penchant for seed heads and pods and fruit. Strawberries are often a favourite, and much damage can be caused by roe to a vegetable patch. On the other hand roe cause little damage to most agricultural crops, other than some root crops in hard winter weather. They are seen in newly brairded cereal crops in spring and in these fields later in the year, but the few young shoots that they eat early in the growth rarely cause much damage to the final yield, and later in the season their food objective is primarily the weed plants growing in the crop.

As with red deer, the roe metabolism, or food requirement or appetite, is reduced in winter, coupled with reduced energy output. The food requirement for adult bucks is less than for does, particularly in late summer and early winter, which explains why the former seem to be less visible during that period. During summer the doe has a high intake requirement to enable her to maintain lactation, and again in spring to provide nutrition for her embryos, and in early winter, even if she has stopped lactating, she will require to build up reserves for hard weather.

Environmental factors govern roe behaviour and activity. The changing daylight lengths, and the quality of available food, which is generally scarce and of poor quality in winter and abundant and high quality in summer. Roe adapt to this situation by their metabolic rate declining in winter. The resorbing area of their rumen shrinks in winter, and its volume decreases by around 20%; which would seem to be an adaptation for energy saving. Research has been carried out into the activity patterns of roe in some areas. These bouts of activity and inactivity are longest in winter, and most of their active time occurs at sunrise and sunset, especially during the winter months.

Research suggests that a variation between activity, moving around and feeding, and inactivity, resting or ruminating, decreases in does about April until June, when there is little evidence of the activity being concentrated at dawn and dusk, presumably as a result of the demands of the foetus and offspring. By July and August there is an increase in discernible peak activity periods again. In August most doe activity is noticed one or two hours after sunrise, whereas in the October-January period this occurs one or two hours after sunset. They are mostly nocturnal in winter, but in December-February, before the appetite reduction period, there is sometimes discernible activity in the afternoons on fine days.

Bucks follow similar patterns, although there is more activity during the July/August rut period. In October and November and February-April they tend to be more active in the evenings, after sunset, than in the mornings.

These observations are generalisations and averages of course, and much depends upon weather, habitat, and idiosyncratic behaviour. Generally in winter there are longer periods of resting and inactivity than activity for roe does, with the latter increasing to more like half the time in summer, whereas bucks tend to rest rather more than 50% of the time throughout the year, and especially so in late winter during the period of reduced appetite. Research has suggested that in a 24 hour period during the first three months of the year there may be around 9 or 10 active bouts, increasing to about 15 in May, and then reducing again towards the end of the year. In areas of disturbance, especially shooting, or where the roe come out to forage in open fields, night time activity is increased.

Ruminants mostly lie down when ruminating, and it is thought that only a comparatively small proportion of the inactive time for both roe and red deer is actually spent asleep. Ruminants tend to eat until their stomach is full, and then lie down to ruminate and digest the food. The better quality and more digestible the food the quicker the rumen empties, and smaller animals tend to have a higher metabolic rate and smaller rumens, and so the cycle of feeding, ruminating and resting tends to be faster. Red deer, being substantially larger, tend to have fewer foraging periods in 24 hours, and perhaps these vary from 5-10. Lactating does obviously need better quality and more food, and their energy intake may increase to more than double that of yeld females.

The apparent requirement for water to drink for roe deer is low. They undoubtedly need water and appreciate this when it is available, but they are able to survive, and thrive, in areas where there is no apparent surface water available to them, such as the North Downs in Surrey for instance, which is a chalk ridge of considerable extent. However they are able to obtain their water requirement from the herbage that they eat, and this is undoubtedly why they favour feeding after rain or a heavy dew when the foliage is wet. Very often a summer evening after a shower of rain is a good time to see roe for this reason.

It is sometimes stated that the growing of antlers by the bucks, and the change to winter coat by the deer, require the animals to draw considerably upon their energy resources, but research does not appear to have substantiated this view unequivocally so far as antler growth is concerned, although at the time of the annual spring moult a significant rise in the metabolic rate of the roe has been recorded. The bucks grow their antlers at a time when they have had ample opportunity to build up reserves after the rut. The change to winter coat in adult roe appears to be rapid. In kids, the change is slower and the white spotted red pelage is gradually changed to winter coat over a period in late summer and early autumn until by early winter their winter coat resembles that of adult deer. Mature roe appear to change to winter attire in a matter of a few days. Contrary to apparent popular opinion and most accounts in literature, roe, like red deer, do not moult in autumn, but the hairs metamorphose, growing longer and hollow, whilst a new supplementary thick layer of grey hair grows through the existing summer coat. One does not see scruffy looking roe with partially shed hair, or find loose shed hair in beds in autumn, as is the case in spring. Logically, of course, it would be an unwise design for an animal to have to risk moulting at a time of year when weather is often inclement. The same change in coat applies to most British mammals. Stalkers who skin deer at this time of year will be familiar with this situation. One theory is that the darker winter coat of deer enables them to absorb more heat.

A factor that is generally taken into consideration when establishing some sort of management plan for roe deer is the territorial behaviour of bucks. Often a 'master buck' theory is postulated, and whilst there may be some element of reality in this idea, mostly the theory expressed is too dogmatic and does not altogether fit in with other data. Theory suggests that adult bucks start to mark territories earlier than juveniles, enabling them to stake out their territory with the psychological advantage of being already in possession of it. The two peaks of fraying activity are interpreted as the initial marking out of their chosen territory for the summer, subsequent to which activity eases off, since, once marked, other bucks will have been banished from the area or will be warned to keep out by the signs. The second fraying peak occurs at rut time, to warn off interloping bucks. After the rut fraying ceases. The 'master buck' theory is that once the large aggressive buck has chased off his rivals, if left in peace he will continue to keep out other bucks from the area, thus reducing the amount of prospective fraying damage to the area.

Known data does not appear to support this idea too strongly. In the first place it is known that roe bucks experience two peaks of testosterone secretion, the first in spring at antler hardening and velvet cleaning time, and the second at the rut time. It is also well established that high testosterone levels in animals causes aggressive behaviour. It is common to watch a buck fraying frantically some small tree when there appears to be no rival in the vicinity. It is also all too frequent that one can find where a buck has clearly gone down a line of young trees fraying one after the other, or perhaps several trees in a group are attacked and damaged. If one watches a buck with newly or partially cleaned antlers fraying a sapling it becomes clear that the sensation and activity of fraying is something that the animal appears to enjoy or give him satisfaction. It would also appear that saplings that exude resin or sap with a strong scent seems to be more attractive. What is clear from such observation is that the buck is motivated by compulsive aggressive activity as a result of the testosterone, and this takes place whether another buck is evident there or not. If another younger buck does appear a chase may well take place, and subsequently the victor may well resort to fraying a tree; but this is more an aggressive manifestation of victory than creating a territorial marking post. Such aggressive behaviour is common to all animals with high testosterone levels. In spring sometimes one can notice the more evident descended and active testicles of a buck, as is apparent at the time of rut later in the summer; both being periods of peak testosterone secretion.

The second point to bear in mind, particularly in relation to management ideas, is the probability of underestimation of the deer population. In other words there are probably many more bucks sharing a particular range than appears evident. There have been attempts at estimating roe populations in Britain, but the most impressive data on this subject emanated from Denmark. The oft quoted example was at the Kalo Biological Research Station, where it was decided to shoot out and replace the entire roe population on the estate. After careful assessment and estimation of numbers a planned shooting operation was carried out. The outcome was that the total of roe shot was three times the professionally previously estimated total population. However, this was only one of several examples, and instances are recorded of several other exercises with similar result. One such was where a 600 hectare fenced woodland area was populated by poor quality roe, and there were thought to be 125 deer within this. They managed to kill a total of 161 deer but there were still some left there. Another instance was the experience of a wooded 200 hectare peninsular judged to contain 60 roe, where these were required to be completely removed. Some months later, after 120 deer had been killed, there were still a lot left. On all of these the careful shooting of the deer resulted in totals exceeding the supposed population by an absurdly large margin.

These experiences suggest that the theoretical idea of a section of ground split up into well marked roe territories carefully guarded by the resident master buck, perhaps tolerating an occasional young beast too, does not conform to the probability of there actually being present far more bucks than realised; and in practice most stalkers familiar with a piece of ground will see from time to time bucks that they have no recollection of seeing previously and probably never see again. In summer roe just do not care for the proximity of other roe and tend to keep their distance from each other. One can see mature bucks sharing the same range, and one can observe a mature buck passing along the same track along which another had passed a few minutes previously, without any sign of reaction of aggression or disquiet at the scent of the other animal.

The Roe Deer Rut

For many stalkers the time of the roe deer rut, in the second half of July and the first half of August, is the most exciting part of the season. As well as the thrill of calling bucks, at this time of year it is often possible to lure old cautious beasts out of thickets in places that normally are difficult to stalk, and to see bucks that one has not seen before. The rutting season takes place at approximately the same time of year throughout Britain, sometimes with perhaps a small variation of a few days earlier in the south and a few days later in the north. There is an idea prevalent, as a result of mention in past literature, that a second, so-called 'false' rut takes place in late autumn, perhaps in early October, and people have reported seeing roe mating then. This idea almost certainly resulted from the belief in the past that since other deer species rut in about October roe must also do so. Research has been carried out into this subject over the past century, and it is clear that after the end of the rut in late August the testosterone level and the ability to produce semen in roe bucks falls off rapidly. A few spermatozoa may remain in the epididymis through September, so theoretically it might be possible for a buck to mate successfully then if a doe that was functioning abnormally was also receptive at that time. How this prospect of a late mating would affect diapause, implantation and birth date is not fully understood, were it to occur, but presumably would result in kids born in August. For practical purpose the idea of a late 'false' rut can be disregarded, although it is conceivable that a yearling doe might come into oestrus late, having failed to do so earlier for some obscure reason, or metabolic malfunction or abnormality, and so attract male attention.

Another misconceived perception relating to the rut is the matter of roe rings. It has been written that roe rings are traditional sites used annually over a long period. It is possible that this is so in unusual circumstances, but for the most part roe rings occur in places where vegetation growth precludes their occurrence in the following year. It may be that in some mature forests, or perhaps a small glen in the hills, a small clearing or open space is frequented by roe, and in such a place a large stone or tree stump or bush might form a pivotal point around which roe will circle to form a ring, and so give rise to this idea. However rutting roe do not all run in circles by any means and roe rings do not occur even in a large percentage of matings. Moreover, if one observes roe running in the rut, with the doe leading on the buck, in suitable conditions, such as long grass, and then subsequently examines the area, it is easy to see that the two deer circling some object, such as a thistle, quickly form a beaten track and they do not need to go round very often to form a roe ring.

During the rut the buck is often referred to as chasing or running the doe. Distinction should be drawn between two types of activity. The first is a very fast chase, when the aggressive buck is actually chasing an unreceptive doe that is clearly not yet in season and ready to stand for mating. In this case the doe is actually trying to get away and elude the unwanted male attention. When the doe is properly coming into season the buck tends to stay close to her keeping a careful watch on her, following as she moves away feeding, or lying close to her. When she is receptive she will move at a quite slow run, with the buck following behind at a similar pace, sometimes with his nose almost at her tail. In this situation it is clear that the doe is leading on the buck, not being chased by him. Sometimes they will run at this slow steady pace for some time, with the doe weaving round objects, occasionally in a circle, sometimes in a figure of eight motion, and sometimes covering quite a distance either back and forth or otherwise, but remaining well within her small territory, where her kid or kids are lying somewhere in cover nearby. When she stops, if she is ready, the buck will mount her; and this procedure may be carried out a number of times. Occasionally, if her kid or kids are present at the time they may run with her.

An understanding of the sexual biology of roe deer helps to explain some of the rutting behaviour, especially in relation to the unusual characteristics of this aspect in the doe. It is a time of periods of frenetic activity on the part of the roe, because the opportunity for successful mating occurs for only a short time. The weather seems to play some part in activity observed. Rather humid thundery weather seems to inspire activity amongst the deer, and cold winds have the opposite effect. In some years stalkers observe much activity amongst the roe at rutting time, and in other seasons very little activity is reported. Nevertheless, even when little sign of the rut is observed it must take place successfully since kids are born normally the following spring.

In Germany the time of the roe rut is sometimes called *blattzeit*, which means leaf time. This is because the traditional method of calling roe amongst old professional hunters was by using a taut beech leaf between the thumbs, blowing upon this to produce the appropriate sound. Numerous artificial roe calls are available on the market and choice is largely a matter of personal opinion, since they all work well at times. Calls where the operator blows on a reed have a slight disadvantage in that sometimes the reed gets affected by saliva after much blowing and requires to be dried before further use. A rubber call rather smaller than a tennis ball, called a Buttolo, has the advantage that this does not occur since the air is blown over the reed by pressure of the hand in squeezing the rounded rubber body of the device. This call gives two notes; the conventional 'fiep' is generated by squeezing the call gently, whereas the *angst-geschrei* call, almost a shriek, is produced by a very hard squeeze.

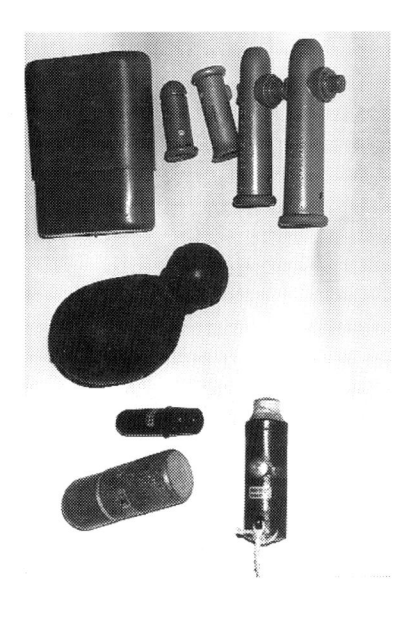

In German hunting parlance there are four specific roe calls: the *kitz* call, the *fiep*, the *sprengfiep* and the *geschrei*. These have particular purposes. The highest tone is the kitz or kid call, and this is used to imitate the cry of a young kid in order to attract a doe. It has been demonstrated that a doe in August that took no notice of the very slightly lower fiep call came running when the tone was raised to the higher pitch of the kid call.

The fiep is the usual tone of roe buck calls and emulates the noise made by the doe when calling or being followed by a buck. The noise made by the doe is very quiet, though probably carries much further to the acute ears of a deer than is apparent to a human. In some woodland where acoustics are good the doe can be heard giving this call, about every second step, as she runs comparatively slowly with a buck following her. The sprengfiep is meant to be the call made by the doe when ready to be mated or being mated. The loudest and lowest call, the geschrei, resembles a shriek. It is sometimes known as an *Angstgeschrei* or cry of terror. This is meant to represent the scream of a doe pursued or approached by an unwanted buck, and is not quite so low in tone as, nor similar to, the scream made by a terrified injured roe. Despite its extraordinary seemingly un-deer-like sound, the geschrei call can be remarkably effective and produce spectacular results on occasion.

Although it is possible to call other deer species, either by imitating their young or by emulating the call of a rival male, the calling of roe deer has been practised more widely than for other species in continental Europe for several centuries. The roe buck does not make aggressive roars or whistles as do some other species of deer, and his vocal reactions are largely limited to a sort of snorting sound sometimes heard when one comes at speed in response to calling. Possibly the reason for the tradition of calling roe, and its importance in roe stalking, sometimes enabling bucks to be lured from impenetrable cover, is that these are solitary animals at rut time rather than herding species, and the period of the rut is comparatively short, whilst the time that the doe is receptive to mating is very limited. Whereas with other deer species, if the female is not successfully mated during her first oestrus she will cycle again, and continue to do so for a number of times, the roe doe is monoestrous; which is to say that she has only one oestrus cycle a year and is only receptive to the mating by the buck for perhaps only a matter of hours. Thus there is urgency about the need to mate at the critical time, and this may explain the attraction of the buck to a call that suggests a receptive doe in the vicinity.

There are various theories about calling roe deer by means of artificial calls and the techniques involved. Without doubt the most effective way for a tyro to gain confidence in this exciting method of enticing bucks into view is to see the procedure successfully demonstrated, and then to achieve success for himself or herself. Once the person has actual experience of the excitement of a roe buck, or even a doe, coming to the call, and realises that it does work, then the confidence is established to try calling in future, even when attempts are not always successful.

Most stalkers seem to be of the opinion that when calling roe one must not do so too frequently. This is probably a sensible view, although if one is able to watch a doe running in front of a buck, or even see a doe standing calling, and is able to hear the small fieping noise that she makes, one is aware that it is uttered continuously for a short period. However, part of the problem with calling roe deer is locating any approaching deer, and being aware of these. Often the animals will approach cautiously, in cover, down wind of the sound in order to scent the originator of the call, and not come rushing towards it as sometimes happens. For this reason there is merit in giving the call four or five times and then waiting quietly for a few minutes, concentrating upon watching and listening for any sound of an animal. Sometimes a roe buck will be seen at a distance and the stalker may well try to call him in closer. If the buck ignores the fiep call, then perhaps the geschrei call may cause him to respond, sometimes at full speed.

Stalkers able to mimic successfully can sometimes attract roe, especially bucks, by barking at the deer, emulating their own bark. Sometimes it is said that older bucks have a deeper voice than young bucks or does, and so differentiation of tone may be of significance; but if opportunity is taken to watch deer barking, both roe bucks and does, or deer of differing age groups, one might question the idea and take the view that voice characteristics are idiosyncratic, and that no differentiation between sexes is discernible.

The various faculties of roe are well developed, particularly their powers of hearing and scent. Sometimes it is possible to have roe walk to within a very short distance of someone standing still and not too obvious, without the deer apparently seeing the person. It may be that their eyesight definition is less good, but it may equally be that the deer is thinking of other things and fails to identify an unmoving object just as happens with humans too. Roe rarely look upwards without reason, and so they will often walk right underneath a high seat and fail to see the observer perched above. However, the noise of a camera being used or a metallic click from a rifle will cause the deer to focus instantly in that direction. Roe have large ears, and put these to good use. In woodland habitat wind direction is less certain, since the breeze may circulate in open spaces and be interrupted or diverted by trees and other cover. The stalker should bear this in mind.

After the rut is over roe bucks often seem to disappear and be seldom seen. This is simply because compared with the does the bucks maintain a low profile. It is not a question of their retiring into cover to recuperate from the rut, since, unlike most herding deer species males, roe bucks do not lose condition significantly at that period. They continue feeding normally and their periods of activity are limited, since their attention is largely confined to just one or two does in their range and the actual length of time involved in great activity is small. However, unlike the does, the bucks do not need to feed more than to maintain their condition plus adding a little reserve for the winter in the form of renal fat. Whereas the does that are milking need to eat sufficient to accommodate this demand as well as maintaining their condition, and though the amount of milk that they produce may seem small, the demand of the production of the milk on their metabolism, as on all mammals, is actually quite significant.

Paint, Pins and Teeth

As with all woodland deer stalking, but especially for roe, which are such small animals, it is important that the stalker either has his own dog, trained to find deer, or has access to one. Quite apart from the critical situation of a wounded beast that has to be followed and despatched, even well shot deer hit in the heart or lungs can, and usually will, run a few yards at least, and may well disappear from view behind some obstacle or into thick cover. A roe deer lying flat and quite dead in even comparatively short grass can be difficult to find, as an experienced stalker will know. So the ability to find signs and trail the animal is important, with the use of a dog as a back up if the trail is difficult to follow.

When shooting deer in woodland it is important to try to mark carefully both the precise spot where the animal stood at the time that the shot was fired, and the spot and angle from which the shot was taken, so that if necessary one can re-construct the scene to facilitate a search for signs, such as for indications of a bullet strike. It is also important to be able to judge from the reaction of the animal, and the signs on the ground, where on the animal the bullet struck, and thus its likely effect. With a heart or lung shot the animal will probably run, rather low, before collapsing dead. If the beast gives a slight jump it may indicate a low shot, and if it stands humped up this indicates a gut shot too far back. If the animal drops on the spot, to a neck or body shot, it should always be approached with caution and the rifle ready, since should the bullet have struck too high it may have felled the animal only temporarily, giving the same effect as being struck on the spine or neck with a heavy stick. If this is the case the deer may recover and rise and run off with a superficial wound. A neck shot severing the vertebrae will fell the animal on the spot, but not necessarily kill it, and a speedy despatch is required by either a second shot, or preferably by use of a knife, 'sticking' it in the throat or heart to bleed it, as described for red deer.

Experience should teach the stalker to recognise reaction to shots and to be able to judge the likely resultant behaviour of the deer. Further information is yielded by what the old venery terms describe as 'paint and pins', the signs of blood and hair at the spot where the animal stood. This is why it is so important to mark and recognise this spot. Once one has moved after the shot, identifying precisely the place where the animal stood becomes more difficult. If two people are present it may be a good idea for one to remain at the point where the shot was taken, in order to direct the other to the judged place of bullet impact. Spots or splashes of blood may indicate, from the colour of this, the site of strike, and any hairs found may confirm this by their colour and texture and length, which may well indicate from which part of the deer's anatomy they came. Familiarity with the different hair on the roe in various parts of the body, derived from examination of carcasses, and particularly from skinning them, is important for attempted recognition of the few hairs that may be cut out by a bullet strike.

Judgement of the age of any animal is imprecise after a certain stage of growth. One has only to try judging the age of a group of people, or indeed their dogs, to appreciate how difficult accuracy can be, and many factors are misleading if they are abnormal, such as early turning grey for instance. So, without the facility for other more scientific aids, in the field or in the larder, reliance has to be made on the basis of experience of the deer in that area, and judgement of age made accordingly. There is little doubt that being able to watch the animal moving about undisturbed enables one to gain an impression as to whether the roe is young, middle-aged, or old.

Many people seem to regard antlers as a guide to age assessment, and to some extent these can give indications, such as thickness or angle of pedicles, but one could easily be fooled by deformed antlers from a beast that one has never seen entire, which may have had some disability that produced abnormal antlers. Equally, gold medal roe buck antlers have been produced by known yearlings, and someone handling the trophy subsequently might never assess the age as being so young. More importantly, many people are keen to label roe bucks with age assessment, but never bother to do so with does.

However it is possible to decide upon the age of roe deer quite precisely up to the age of about three years old. The rate of tooth growth of roe is faster than that of red deer, which may not be surprising because they are smaller animals with probably shorter life spans. Consequently tooth replacement is completed by the age of one and a half years. After that the cannon bone in the leg gives a guide, since at two and a half years the epiphysis, or the small joint on the end of this, becomes fused Thereafter one has to rely upon subjective judgement of tooth wear as the main aid to judging age, bearing in mind whilst doing so that this can be dependent not only on the type of food eaten, but on idiosyncratic tooth performance.

YEARLING ROE DEER
May

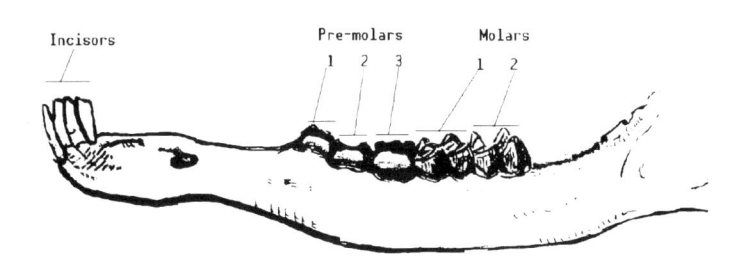

Deer have two basic types of teeth, cutting ones and grinding ones. The former are the incisors at the front of the jaw and exist only on the bottom jaw, biting on to a hard gum pad above, whilst the grinding teeth are molars and are present on both upper and lower jaws of course, to enable food to be ground between them. Deer use these molars as well to bite off harder foliage, or plants, such as twigs. In a full set of adult teeth there are four pairs of incisors, or eight teeth, and six molars on each side of the lower jaw. The front three are referred to as pre-molars and the back three as molars. Some people refer to the outside pair of incisors, the smallest, as the eye teeth.

The roe kid starts off with four pairs of milk incisors, and at six months old the central pair is replaced by a pair of larger permanent ones. A month later the next pair is replaced, with the third at around nine months old and the eye teeth becoming permanent ones at around ten months. Thereafter incisor teeth are no longer a reliable age guide. They may become very worn with age in some cases, or more likely they may simply fall out, as is the case with old sheep. The incisors can be worn down to resemble little round pearls, and some deer may have some or all missing. A fairly young buck has been recorded with no incisors at all. He was not in particularly good condition and had poor antlers and undoubtedly there was a connection between these factors.

A roe kid initially has only three milk pre-molars. When the molars appear, these are permanent teeth, and the first emerges at about four months old, whilst the second erupts at about six months. Between eight and ten months the permanent pre-molars start appearing, pushing off the milk teeth. It is worth noting that the third pre-molar has three cusps in milk form, or in the first tooth, but only two cusps as a permanent tooth. Between ten months and a year old the stained milk pre-molars can be seen being pushed off by the white permanent ones, and at about a year old these finally disappear leaving white unstained pre-molars. These gradually become darker and by about August of the animal's second year have become stained.

YEARLING ROE DEER
June

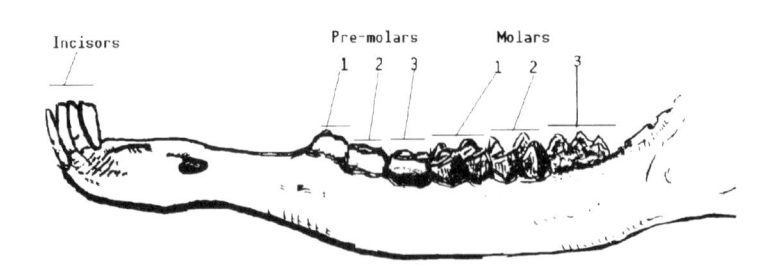

The third molar, the back tooth, which is three cusped, appears at about thirteen months. This starts off white, with the back cusp smaller, and remains quite sharp and unworn until the deer is about one and a half years old, by which time it is starting to stain as the first and second molars are by that stage.

From time to time very small runt roe bucks are shot and it is interesting to check upon such deer, bucks or does, that appear abnormally under-sized, to try to establish age. Some people speculate about an autumn false rut with roe deer, and it would be interesting to establish whether any of these abnormally small beasts are actually conceived later, assuming, of course, that tooth eruption in an abnormal beast is normal, in order to establish whether in fact some unusual happening occurred, such as a doe coming into oestrus remarkably late in the season and associating with a buck that had retained some functional sperm in its epididymis, or some abnormal happening occurred with the implantation, or indeed whether the animal was simply a runt, as occur with most animals occasionally.

Assessment of the age of mature roe is rather subjective, but the relative wear of the teeth and the colour and size of the dentine band exposed by the grinding down of the molars gives a comparative guide in most cases. Nevertheless, even comparison with a series of jaws, thought to be of differing ages and representative, has to be considered subjectively, taking into account any other factors, especially the overall appearance of the animal and also its environment.

Although checking the judgement of tooth wear and age assessment from this is possible with farmed red deer of known ages, this is not practical with roe deer, unless a large number of tagged kids, and recorded ages of these at death, are available in order that a sufficient sample of sectioned teeth can be examined and wear compared. Until such data is available one should bear in mind that a study by the National Veterinary Laboratory in Stockholm with sectioned teeth from roe of known ages at death, resulting from deliberately tagged kids, suggested that tooth section examination was not reliable for age assessment, since results indicated ages almost double the known ages, and tooth wear was judged to be a more accurate form of measure.

It is a good idea for a stalker to get into the habit of looking for points of unusual interest when handling deer carcasses, such as wounds, illness or abnormalities. When gralloching and cutting out the rectum it is necessary to lift the tiny tail of the roe, and in doing so it should be obvious if this is abnormally long. A good habit to adopt also is that of running a finger over both sides of the upper jaw to check for vestigial canine teeth or tusks. In roe these appear as merely a tiny sharp or hard protuberance through the gum of the jaw. It has been suggested that vestigial canine teeth occur in up to 6% of roe in some countries, but it is likely that in Britain the occurrence is far lower than this; perhaps as low as 1%, and it is rarer still to find an animal showing a pair of these tiny tusks. They may occur in both bucks and does, but are more commonly found in the former; perhaps because more attention is paid to the teeth of these.

Gralloching woodland roe deer differs from that of hill red deer in that it is best to completely remove all entrails and ensure cooling of the carcass as rapidly as possible. If the heart and lungs are to be removed there is no necessity for bleeding the animal, since all blood will be removed with the gralloching anyway. This is most easily achieved, both gralloch removal and cooling, by opening up the carcass completely, cutting up through the rib cage centrally. Some continental stalking knives are provided with a saw blade for this purpose, but with a strong sharp knife this is not necessary. The best knives for the purpose are straight-bladed non-folding, with the shaft of the metal forming the blade passing up completely through the handle to ensure strength. There is no need for a large knife. A four inch blade, or even three inch, is sufficient, with a four inch handle.

Having carefully cut off the penis and testicles of a buck, or the udder off a doe, without piercing the stomach cavity, a small slit can be made in the latter near the pelvis, and two fingers inserted. The point of the knife, with the blade held horizontally to avoid puncturing organs, can then carefully be run up guided between the two fingers, to open the stomach cavity up to the breast bone. The skin should then be cut up the centre of the rib cage to the throat. Then, using the weight of the carcass, the knife can be inserted under the breast bone and the rib cage can be cut open centrally up to the gullet by means of several sharp thrusts. Once the whole body cavity is open, removal of the contents is comparatively easy. The gullet should be cut, and severing connective tissue, the whole gralloch can be removed; but first the rectum should be cut loose by running the knife around this externally through the pelvic arch. This and the bladder can then carefully be taken out through the body cavity, and the rest of the organs removed, and the carcass placed on its front to drain out any blood. The liver, kidneys, heart, and other organs required to be saved, for human or canine consumption, can be cut from the gralloch and placed in a plastic bag. The unwanted part of the gralloch should then be hidden in undergrowth or disposed of carefully.

The most satisfactory and cleanest method of carrying a roe carcass, especially where these are likely to be infested with ticks, is a proper roe bag. Rucksacks with waterproof linings are often used for this purpose, but these have the disadvantage of positioning the roe carcase further down the back than a purpose made roe carrying sack as shown below. Made from strong waterproof material, this bag is easily washed clean. The carcass is simple to secure inside it, and the whole package sits well up on the shoulders to ease the burden of carrying.

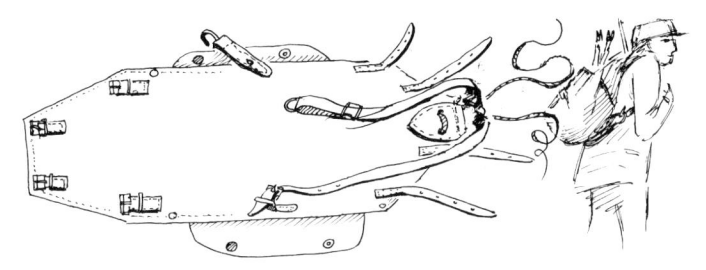

The carcass, once back in the larder should be hung by it back legs, with a stick propping open the body cavity to facilitate cooling. The optimum period for hanging the roe depends upon the facility and temperature of the larder, the weather, and personal taste. However, during the midsummer rutting period, when the weather is likely to be warm, and possibly even thundery, unless the larder is modern with a cooling plant to maintain a low temperature, probably four or five days is quite sufficient, and three days may be long enough in sultry weather before skinning and butchering takes place. It is important to take precautions to prevent access by flies, which can be a great nuisance in summer.

An interesting point concerning the anatomy of roe deer and the number of pairs of ribs is that occasionally these are found to differ. Professor Karl Borg of the State Institute of Veterinary Medicine in Stockholm some years ago was asked by the police to examine a roe carcass, of a deer that was suspected of being poached, to advise on the location of the wound. He noticed during his examination that this animal had 14 pairs of ribs rather than the normal 13 pairs. Subsequent research revealed that about 8% of roe bucks and 11.9% of does differed from the normal 13 pairs, and the number of lumbar vertebrae differed from the norm of 6, and in 4.7% of bucks and 6.3% of does rudimentary canine teeth (or tusks) were found, either one or a pair.

Roe Does

The culling of roe does is an important part of managing the deer population, and, as with hind stalking, can be as exciting from the point of view of the actual stalking as the pursuit of bucks, if less glamorous with no trophy at the culmination. As with hind stalking, achieving the target female cull in the season available can be a challenge. This because not only is the weather in winter less conducive, but the days are short and the roe largely nocturnal in habit. Consequently success is easier in the early part of the doe season.

However, in places where achieving required doe cull numbers proves difficult it is often worth considering undertaking a moving operation with the assistance of several competent stalkers. This involves a person, or perhaps two people, walking slowly downwind zigzagging through the woodland so as to disturb the roe by his or her scent, or that of an accompanying dog, but without pushing the deer forward too quickly. One or two rifles judiciously positioned at a clearing or ride in the wood, preferably in high seats, where the downward angle of a shot is safer, as well as giving better opportunity to study the deer before taking a careful shot, may then be able to take some does even in the middle of the day. If the deer are moved quietly and unhurriedly forward in the direction of the rifles, hopefully when they come to the ride or opening where these are waiting the animals will pause before crossing the open area and give the rifle a chance to identify the sex of the deer and choose a shot. It is important to bear in mind that early in the season antlers in velvet may not be distinguishable on bucks that have recently shed their antlers, or on kids, and tushes may not easily be seen, and so sex distinction may be less easy.

The choice of which does to cull is not easy, since judgement of age and condition when on the hoof is difficult, and most does are likely to have a kid or kids with them. The prominent anal tush is the obvious distinguishing mark of the female roe in winter coat, and may be easier to detect than the penile tush on the belly of bucks and buck kids. In most cases it is probably a question of culling sufficient does without being too specific as to choice, even if this is available. If a doe is shot, an effort should be made to take also her kid or kids too. Although by late December many does will have ceased lactation, and in good habitat well grown kids may be strong enough to survive as orphans, nevertheless the unquantifiable, but vital, factor of 'motherly love' may make the difference between the survival of the kids or not in hard conditions. Hence the bonding of the roe families until these split up in spring. Rather than leave the orphaned kid where its survival may be judged to be precarious it is more humane to shoot the kid first.

The possible length of a roe doe's lactation period has not been properly researched. Certainly does with udders full of milk have been found in late December, and there is little doubt that some continue milking until well into the winter. One authority has suggested that the roe lactation period varies between 162-194 days. On what data this estimate was based is not known. However the latter figure would take a kid born on June 1st to mid December, and a kid born in mid June (perhaps in the north) to late December.

In undisturbed areas roe can often be found feeding at midday on fine days in winter, especially early in the season when they are still milking and have a high food requirement, and it is always worth looking for them in these conditions as well as at the more traditional dawn and dusk stalking periods. It is often possible to call a roe doe too, using the *kitz* or kid call, and sometimes sitting in a high seat on a quiet evening calling at intervals will attract a doe.

As with red deer, the roe deer are primarily a matriarchal species. That is to say, the doe takes most of the initiative. It is the doe that establishes a summer territory, in which to give birth to, and raise, her kid. This is generally a smaller area than the summer range adopted by a buck, which may overlap more than one doe territory. Moreover the biology of roe, unique amongst deer, dictates the life cycle of both sexes.

Roe does, like red deer hinds, and indeed other species too, remember, or have an affinity with, the place where they gave birth previously, and if undisturbed will return to the same place in subsequent years to have their kids. In some parts of the country they may not move far from this place in winter if there is adequate food and shelter and no disturbance, but in less congenial areas in the north, where winters are harder and food and cover less abundant, roe tend to move into neighbouring woodland, especially conifer woodland that provides good shelter, during winter, and only return to more open ground in summer. In other areas of open agricultural land where winter is less severe the roe may do the opposite, forming groups, perhaps with two or three families together, and staying out in the middle of large fields where they are safer, much like the 'field roe' encountered in continental Europe. A mature doe is usually the leader of these groups.

Most mammals seek temporary privacy when parturition occurs. Herd animals tend to go off to have their offspring, but return to the herd accompanied by the youngster, sometimes within a couple of days, and sometimes a little longer. Plains antelope, such as wildebeest, require that their offspring join the herd and its comparative protection as quickly as possible, but red deer calves and their dams may not join up with others and reform a group until a week or two old, depending upon habitat. The roe doe prefers solitude throughout summer and the period of raising her kids and does not favour the presence of other deer until winter and change of both food type and habit.

Where a doe can be recognised with comparative certainty, by particular caudal marking, or some other characteristic, she may be identified as the animal to have taken up residence in that particular place in previous summers. If cover and food availability is abundant the territory assumed by the doe may be quite small; perhaps only an acre or two. Particularly when the kid or kids are young she will not move far and will keep an eye on where the offspring are hidden. It is often stated that the doe, or the red deer hind, carefully hides her young, placing them in some spot of cover whilst she wanders off feeding. This is not the case. The initiative is invariably taken by the kid or calf. Of course this is logical, as already noted with red deer calves, because it would be unwise for the adult deer to leave a tell-tale scent track up to the comparatively scentless young for some predator to find. Observation will show that when it has suckled, or a short time afterwards, the young deer will turn away from its mother and go and choose a suitable concealed resting place and lie down there. The mother will watch where it goes and know the spot.

Similarly, when the dam returns to her youngsters in order to suckle them, she will stand a little way off from where they are hidden and call softly to them. In the case of roe kid twins, these will lie separately, sometimes quite some distance from each other. The young deer will emerge at her call and come to her to be suckled and groomed. Sometimes, where roe kids are lying well apart in almost differing habitat the doe will visit and suckle each separately.

As the kids consume more solid food, after a few weeks, they begin to accompany the doe for longer periods; but they do not do so continually until late in the summer. By which time the dappling of white spots on their first coats has begun to disappear, with the juvenile pelage gradually being replaced by their longer darker first winter hair.

In good habitat roe does produce twins normally, and in excellent conditions of abundant food and favourable weather triplets are not uncommon. On the other hand in less favourable areas of northern Britain, with winter conditions that are more severe and food supply then more difficult, single kids are more frequent. As with sheep, roe are actually capable of producing multiple kids upon occasion. In Sweden, where, unlike in Britain, interest in roe has been sufficient that research has taken place, and records exist going back to 1947, these show that with a very large number of samples from roe deer found dead from a variety of reasons, including road casualties, predation and disease, totalling 4168 roe of both sexes altogether, pregnant roe does totalling 500 were found to carry an average of just over 2 foeti, with a significant number carrying twins. These Swedish records show that 6 of the does examined between March and mid May were actually carrying 4 foeti, and indeed three does (plus two more in Norway) were recorded as being reported to carry as many as five foeti. Of the 6 deer examined and showing 4 quite large foeti each, three of the does were killed by dogs and one by a lynx. These were probably rather heavy and slow and so easier prey.

Although these multiple foeti were being carried well on towards their term, their ultimate survival would have been an altogether different situation. It might be possible for a heavy milking doe in ideal conditions to rear four kids, but the probabilities are strongly against this, and more than triplets being reared successfully would be extremely unlikely.

One of these heavily pregnant deer was judged to be at least 8 years old, as indeed were a significant number of those pregnant casualties examined, indicating that roe does can breed until at least that age and quite possibly older. The longevity of roe in the wild is not really known, but it is probable that they can live until at least ten and perhaps twelve years in good habitat. The study of roe in wild or simulated wild conditions is not easy because of their solitary preference, and because being so small they are not easily seen in preferred habitat. This is demonstrated by the significant under-estimation of population numbers. Detailed observation of roe in a suitable doe territory sized enclosure of several acres, with plenty of cover, would be difficult, and extrapolation of experience of roe kept in a small area would have to be regarded with suspicion.

Suckling of the kids takes place with reducing frequency as these grow, and in mid summer is probably three times a day at most, reducing to twice a day by late summer. Twins suckling in mid June were noted to suckle the doe for $2^1/_2$ minutes, with one kid taking a further $^1/_2$ minute from behind the doe. It is not known how long lactation takes place, largely because such detail has neither been recorded nor collated from culled does. Indeed many stalkers are unaware even of the number of teats carried by female deer, let alone observing their lactation state. Like sheep, deer have four functional teats (all Cervids have four teats except Musk deer), and at the end of lactation the udder regresses such that by late winter it is no longer visible, especially amongst long winter hair. Just before parturition, sometimes several days or even a couple of weeks before, does being somewhat idiosyncratic in this respect as with domestic livestock, the udder swells and becomes very obvious. A full udder can be observed protruding slightly behind the line of the back of the hind legs in profile view. The size of the udder drops off progressively through the summer and by mid summer is less obvious in a live doe.

Precise details of the complete mechanism of roe pregnancy are not yet known, because sufficient numbers of these deer have not been studied and creditable samples of data gleaned, contrary to the situation in red deer, where detailed research in many parts of the world has revealed much information. However various experiments and research point towards some answers. The roe deer rut in Britain is reckoned to occur from about mid July to mid August, and possibly a few days later in northern Britain. Much of the activity witnessed at the beginning of the rut is that of bucks with high testosterone levels chasing unwilling does not yet in season. The spread of actual mating and conception may well be within a two or three week period. The birth of kids has been recorded at the end of April and early May, but most kids in Britain are born probably during the second half of May and the first week or so in June, with a few a little later, perhaps, in the north. Mean parturition dates have been suggested as May 15th in France, May 21st for Norway, June 1st for West Germany with June 9th for East Germany, and June 2nd and June 14th for two different areas of Denmark.

The gestation period of most mammals is fixed within small limits, and is in proportion to the size of dam and neonate. With red deer, and large numbers held on farms and experimentally over the years, where actual conception dates could be witnessed and recorded, building up a scale of foetus measurement relative to age has been possible. In fact in placental mammals there is a linear relationship between the cube-root of foetal weight and gestational age, but sufficient roe data is not available yet to construct a scale as for red deer. As a rough guide, Swedish records suggest that for roe the average foetal length is 20mm in January, 50mm in February, 100mm in March, 170mm in April and 250mm in May when these are mature. However, in order to calculate back to provide implantation dates a much more precise list of measurements is required, as is available for red deer foeti.

Given that implantation dates for roe must vary in line with the different parturition dates, and that conception dates vary by a week or two through the rut, it appears that the diapause period is a constant period, similar to the gestation period after implantation. This means that the parturition date must be influenced by the date of conception. It appears that day length and melatonin secretion are likely to be involved in influencing the initiation of the oestrus cycle and ovulation, and thus conception, and to act idiosyncratically on the does. Research data has recorded that by subjecting roe does to extended photoperiod alteration with long daylight hours, over a long time (several years), and also by melatonin implants, the oestrus was advanced significantly, resulting in earlier parturition, which appeared to confirm a constant ten month period of diapause and gestation, thus indicating a fixed period of diapause as well as that of the gestation period. There were theories that the winter solstice and the lengthening days, or rather shortening nights, and the consequent change in melatonin secretion, might trigger the blastocyst or egg, free floating in the uterus during diapause, to start the implantation process. However, with the constant length of diapause it would now seem that although the free floating blastocyst appears to change little over the five months of diapause, in fact microscopic changes must be taking place with a small amount of mitosis, or cell division, finally leading to the elongation of the trophoblast and implantation and attachment to the endometrium, or uterus wall; at which time an increase in hormone secretion takes place.

Recently recorded dates of mating and parturition with captive roe does have confirmed a normal pregnancy period, including both diapause and gestation after implantation, of 290 days, with the probable usual idiosyncratic variation by a day or two.

The roe deer is unique amongst ungulates in displaying both delayed implantation and monoestry. Although the latter has been suspected for some years, proof, as a result of research, was only established comparatively recently. Monoestry, which occurs with embryonic diapause in seals also, and is a mechanism whereby mating and parturition both take place at favourable periods, means a single oestrus cycle. Although the occurrence of this in roe is accepted in several continental countries, it seems not to be well known in Britain.

Embryonic diapause, or delayed implantation, was discovered in roe as long ago as 1841, but its significance was not fully appreciated until 1854, when a curious biologist wondered why the gestation period of roe was so long in comparison to their size, and appeared to be ten months as opposed to a predicted five months. A long list of mammals of great variety is now known to exhibit embryonic diapause, including bears, badgers, stoats, otters, armadillos, some mice and so on. This acts in somewhat different ways with varying species. In roe deer the blastocyst, or fertilised egg floats free in the uterus, showing no growth until just before implantation takes place prior to which a slight elongation occurs.

Monoestry in roe was suspected in the early 1980's or before then, but not actually demonstrated until a few years ago. The fact that the roe doe may only be in season for a period of a few hours each year, depending upon the animal and circumstances, is significant in understanding behaviour at rutting time, and explains the sometimes remarkable response to calling bucks. As with much in life, sunlight or daylight is the governing influence. In this case day length is the factor, or more properly night length, which affects the pineal gland causing the secretion of a hormone melatonin during darkness, which in turn affects the secretion of other hormones. These result in the production of an egg, or ovum, and subsequently ovulation, when this egg is released to await fertilisation. A yellow body, or corpus luteum is formed at the site from which the egg is shed, and this secretes yet another hormone called progesterone, the function of which is to maintain pregnancy. In most animals, if there is no fertilisation of the ovum this corpus luteum regresses and disappears, and the cessation of the progesterone secretion allows the oestrus cycle to recommence. It has been found that in the case of roe does the corpora lutea (plural, since several eggs are usually produced at once), do not regress even if no fertilisation occurs, for instance in the complete absence of a buck, and remain, possibly even until spring.

This situation explains why, unlike with other deer species, the roe deer rut is brief, and ceases completely by late August, with the bucks apparently disappearing, and why roe kids are not occasionally discovered born very late, as occurs in other species. It also demonstrates the impossibility of a false rut in autumn, which some people claim to occur. As already explained, by then the testosterone level of the buck will have fallen and sperm production will have ceased long since. Of course oddities occur from time to time with all animals and so one has to be careful not to be overly pedantic. However bucks seen to be excessively interested in does, and even mounting them, occasionally in autumn, may have other explanations, perhaps due to hormone malfunction in some way in one of the animals. On the other hand, as explained, the spring testosterone rise in roe bucks at antler hardening and velvet cleaning time leads to both aggressive behaviour, chasing, fraying activity, and to interest in does that do not reciprocate.

Foxes are the main predator of roe kids, although marauding dogs undoubtedly also kill some. Foxes have been observed catching and carrying off a young kid, one of twins, when the mother was unable to defend both. Adult roe can be aggressive to foxes and clearly do not like them. A doe would be quite capable of delivering a severe blow to a fox with her forefeet, and most foxes would not be tempted to stand up to aggression from a roe, but a young kid discovered resting would be easy prey, being no bigger than a lamb. Mortality of kids is not well researched, but undoubtedly significant numbers die in winter or early spring, particularly in northern Britain. Diseases such as pneumonia are found in roe and probably account for kid losses, as do liver fluke infections. In more congenial conditions in southern Britain these problems are less prevalent, and, together with greater fecundity, this explains the ability of populations to expand easily.

Much is written of the yearling roe being chased off by the doe in spring, and also driven away by bucks establishing territories, but this may be a misinterpretation of the situation. Without doubt adolescents of all species reach a stage where they are inclined to 'do their own thing' and seek independence. This occurs with roe too, particularly buck yearlings, and it is likely that the majority of these take the initiative in wandering off from the doe to seek pastures new. Such is probably Nature's design to avoid inbreeding. Young roe can be seen being chased by adults in spring, but generally it will not be known whether these young deer are actually related to the adult. Much of the chasing is simply that after the break-up of winter groups roe become decidedly anti-social and solitary, and seek a summer residence free from intrusion; but some of the chasing is clearly what one might regard as a form of play and without apparent aggression. Moreover, changes in habitat seasonally, forestry operations, agricultural variation, and so on, may cause adult roe to wander and seek new summer homes too.

Home Smoking

Before the days of refrigeration and freezing of food, surplus meat and fish were preserved for later use by salting and smoking. Even in recent times people in remoter parts of Scotland without electricity salted down mutton for winter supplies and packed herrings into barrels of salt. Modern technologies render such preservation of food no longer necessary, but the attraction of smoked food these days is the flavour. Most people are familiar with smoked haddock, kippers and smoked salmon. Smoked mackerel, trout and eels are widely available, and smoked venison is increasingly obtainable. Of course the most obvious of smoked foods are pork products, bacon and ham. However it is when you buy these latter that it is apparent that smoking itself is not the preservation process, since bacon is available smoked or unsmoked.

Many people probably detect little difference between the taste of bacon that is sold in supermarkets as smoked or unsmoked, but home smoked bacon is altogether different, and none of that milky liquid oozes from the rashers when these are cooked in the frying pan or under the grill, or these days in the microwave oven perhaps. Home cured smoked bacon is full of taste: indeed it is as full of taste as you care to make it. Home smoked venison, red deer or roe, is also delicious, and keeps well. It should be sliced thin like Parma ham.

Curing and smoking food is remarkably easy and does not require expensive equipment, and really takes up little time. In the case of fish the curing is a quick process and only takes a few hours. It is astonishing that more people with availability of fresh fish or venison, or even mutton, do not try smoking their own food, and benefit from the additional alternative flavours and ways of serving these.

It is important to understand the curing process and to appreciate that cold smoking is quite different from hot smoking; the latter being effectively an alternative cooking procedure. The object of salting is to replace moisture in the meat or fish with salt by osmosis, and this prevents the growth of bacteria that might spoil the food. Too little salt absorbed will not give adequate protection, but too much salt will make the meat hard and too salty for most tastes. Larger pieces of meat or fish take longer to cure than smaller ones, and very thick joints, especially ones containing bones, such as a ham or a haunch of venison, are too thick too absorb the brine adequately to the centre, and so this has to be injected into the meat along the bone to ensure proper penetration. An alternative is to simply bone out the joint which simplifies the process and obviates brine injection.

Once the meat has been cured by salting or brining, the subsequent smoking assists further drying of the meat and adds some preservative chemicals, and imparts flavour to the food. It is essential that the smoke reaching the food should be cool. If it is hot, then it will simply have the effect of partially cooking the meat and produce an altogether different product, that is neither cold smoked, nor hot smoked and properly cooked. The cooling of the smoke is easily achieved by hanging the food at sufficient distance from the fire. Some people smoke their food in an old shed, or use an old disused outside privvy, which is tall and narrow and a good shape. The fire is lit on the ground and the meat and fish are hung on a rail just below the roof, with holes drilled in the eaves, to let out the fumes. One can also use an old whisky barrel, with meat hung from a rail across the top of it, but an old 40 gallon drum would do if well cleaned.

The top and bottom of the barrel are removed and it is sited into a cement base on a small mound, with a chimney of old clay field drainage pipes, lightly buried, running up from a small fireplace at the bottom of the mound into the centre of the base. A length of nine feet of pipes, covered in soil, is sufficient to cool the smoke by the time that it enters the barrel. Cover the top of the barrel with an old damp sack, which serves to let the smoke out slowly. In wet weather put a lid over this, slightly raised to allow the smoke to escape below it. Many people seem to have the idea that it is necessary to use oak sawdust for smoking, but this is nonsense. Any available hardwood will do. The important thing is not to use softwoods that might impart resinous flavouring. Many west coast smoking places use oak because scrub oak is the most easily available hardwood along some of the sea lochs, but birch has always been used traditionally in Scotland, and has been shown to be as satisfactory as any other hardwood. Commercial smokeries have carried out experiments and shown that, with differing types of product, varieties of hardwood do not actually impart noticeably differing flavours, and that although smoking hams with apple wood or adding juniper when smoking salmon sounds attractive it actually makes little difference to the taste. Chippings and sawdust that are a by-product from cutting of firewood with a chainsaw and circular saw can be used, and this serves as an admirable way to dispose of the accumulated chips at the wood pile.

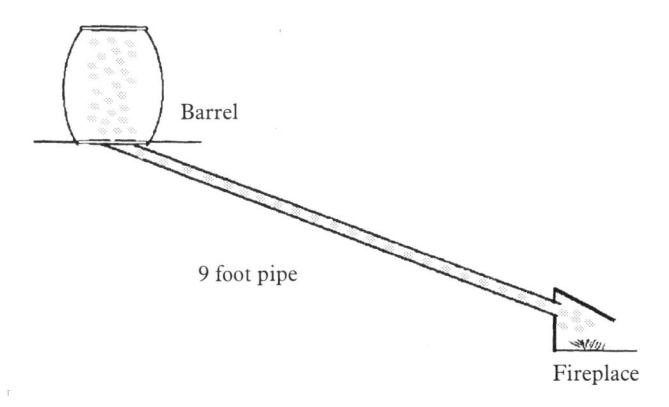

```
        Barrel

              9 foot pipe

                              Fireplace
```

Curing in a brine solution is much easier than using dry salt, and involves little work. For small amounts of food, such as two small roe haunches, a plastic bucket is a suitable container, and for a larger operation use a plastic dustbin.

A different brine is used for salting meat than for fish, and saltpetre (potassium nitrate) is added for the former, as this helps to retain the pink colour of the meat and inhibit bacteria. Without saltpetre the meat turns an unattractive brown colour. The basic brine ingredients are salt and sugar, dissolved in water. Other flavourings are added. The salt hardens the meat and the sugar helps to counteract this and soften it and also to colour it. Many different recipes exist for the proportions and dilution of these brining ingredients, and results depend upon the timing of the immersion. However the following is fine for venison as well as other meat.

Sweet Pickle Brine for Meat
1 gallon water
1lb. salt
4oz sugar (white or brown)
$1/4$oz saltpetre
1oz mixed pickling spice
1 clove crushed garlic

This recipe can be used proportionally to make up whatever quantity of liquid is required to cover the meat in the container. Other herbs or spices can be added to taste.

The salt, sugar and saltpetre are dissolved in the water. Use a little warm water first to facilitate this and then add cold, to ensure that the solution is cool before the meat is added. The crushed garlic can then be added. The pickling spices are simmered in a saucepan containing a half pint of water for half an hour, and then the solids are strained off and the liquid added to the brine.

Once the brine solution is cool the meat is packed into this, ensuring that it does not float to the surface, perhaps by placing a heavy plate or similar on top to keep it submerged. The mixture should be stirred once a day to ensure that all the pieces of meat are properly exposed to the brine. Curing takes three days to the pound for a venison haunch. This timing is based upon the weight of each individual piece of meat, so that small pieces are removed from the brine earlier than larger pieces.

After curing, the pieces of meat are removed from the brine and washed in running water and then hung up for several days in a cool airy place to allow them to dry and the salt to spread evenly. Large pieces of meat can be hung for two or three weeks before smoking. Once boned out haunches are basically dry, after a day or two, they can be trussed into shape by binding with string and then allowed to continue to hang. Venison can be spiced before trussing by rubbing the meat thoroughly in a seasoning made from a mixture of a tablespoonful each of onion powder, garlic powder, paprika, ground black pepper and ground white pepper.

Once the meat is dry it can be smoked. It is best to light the fire beforehand and get this smoking well first, to ensure that the heat from the fire has faded. Either light a small fire of kindling wood in the fireplace and then add chainsaw chips or sawdust gradually until it is smouldering well, or simply place a heap of dry chips into the fireplace and insert a lighted gas poker into these until they are smouldering properly. The smoking time is arbitrary, but generally allow somewhere between 24 and 48 hours. This need not be continuous and it does not matter if the fire goes out during the night.

Rifles for Deer

The legislation currently differentiates between England and Wales and Scotland. South of the Border rifles must be at least of .240 calibre and fire a soft or hollow nosed bullet giving muzzle energy of at least 1700 ft. lbs.

In Scotland rifles for roe deer shooting must have a muzzle velocity of at least 2450 ft/sec. and muzzle energy of 1000 ft. lbs. firing a bullet of 50 grains weight or more. This means that for roe a centre fire .222 rifle is legal. For other deer species the muzzle velocity specified is at least 2450 ft/sec. and a muzzle energy of 1750 ft. lbs. with a bullet weight of 100 grains or over. Effectively this means a .243 calibre, or larger, qualifies.

Shooting Seasons for Deer

Species	Sex	England and Wales	Scotland
Red deer	Stags	August 1st-April 30th	July 1st-October 20th
	Hinds	Nov. 1st-Feb. 29th	Oct. 21st-Feb. 15th
Sika	Stags	August 1st-April 30th	July 1st-October 20th
	Hinds	Nov. 1st-Feb. 29th	Oct. 21st-February 15th
Fallow	Bucks	August 1st-April 30th	August 1st-April 30th
	Does	Nov. 1st-Feb. 29th	October 21st-Feb.15th
Roe	Bucks	April 1st-October 30th	April 1st-October 20th
	Does	Nov. 1st-February 29th	October 21st-March 31st

Muntjac – no close season

CHASING THE RED DEER AND FOLLOWING THE ROE

Deerstalking Calendar

	January	February	March	April	May	June	July	August	September	October	November	December
Red Deer												
Stag-Eng.								1st →				30th Apr
Stag-Scot.							1st			20th		
Hind-Eng.											1st →	
Hind-Scot.		15th								21st		
Fallow												
Buck-Eng.								1st				
Buck-Scot.				1st						20th		
Doe-Eng.											1st	
Doe-Scot.		15th								21st		
Sika												
Stag-Eng.								1st				
Stag-Scot.							1st			20th		
Hind-Eng.											1st	
Hind-Scot.		15th								21st		
Roe Deer												
Buck-Eng.				1st								
Buck-Scot.				1st						20th		
Doe-Eng.											1st	
Doe-Scot.										21st		
Muntjac	No close season
Chinese Water Deer	No close season

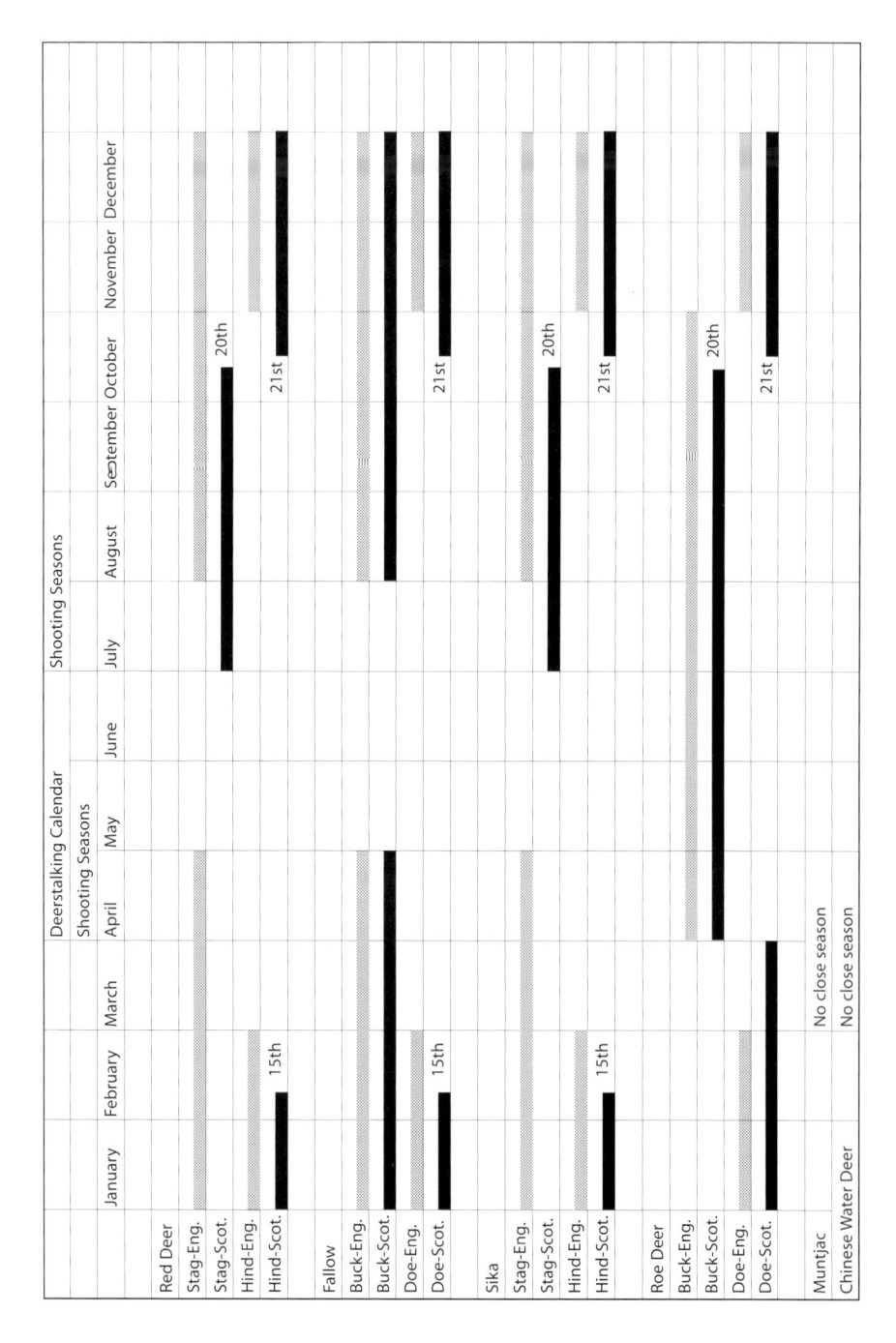

128

Lyme Disease

In most parts of Britain deer of all species are host to ticks, and in some areas they are infested with them. As a result, deerstalkers are prone to find themselves becoming temporary host to occasional ticks, particularly after handling deer carcasses. Mostly ticks only are an irritation, resulting in a tiresome itch that may last for a day or two after removing one of the creatures that becomes attached. Removal should be done carefully to avoid leaving the head imbedded in the skin. However, stalkers, and others visiting the countryside or handling deer in tick resident areas, should be aware of Lyme disease, which is one of the tick-borne diseases that affects humans.

The disease is named after Lyme in Connecticut, where an outbreak occurred a few years ago, subsequent to which the hitherto unknown spirochaete *Borrelia burgdorferi* was identified. One of the problems is that many of the symptoms are non-specific, and so diagnosis may not correctly identify the cause. Not all people bitten by ticks and infected by the disease exhibit the characteristic "bulls-eye rash", Erythema migrans, which is a red ring with a pale centre.

Symptoms include feeling as if one has contracted 'flu, joint pains, headaches or neck stiffness, and arthritis-like condition. The disease can cause fatigue and M E-like symptoms. A severe case can result in facial paralysis or palsy, meningitis and encephalitis.

A further problem is that tests for Lyme disease are not completely reliable either in connection with positive or with negative results. If a stalker should experience any of these symptoms that cannot otherwise be explained it is worth considering the possibility of a tick bite having caused Lyme disease, since even the tiny pin head sized nymphs can transmit the disease, and such might not be noticed, even if they did bite.

Tick bloated with blood, compared to £1 coin and airgun pellets.

INDEX

anal tush, 115
angle of a shot, 23
antlers, 9, 12, 35-41, 52-54, 57, 59, 69, 72, 76-78, 80, 85-89, 93, 94, 97, 108, 114
appetite, 35, 42, 43, 71, 86, 91, 95, 96
barking, 105
binoculars, 17, 18, 74, 91
bipods, 20, 21
birth, 39, 60, 67-70, 101, 115, 119
black roe, 29, 94
blastocyst, 120
bleaching, 54
blood, 31-33, 39, 50, 57, 108, 112
bones, 63, 77, 78
bore sighter, 26
calling, 48, 101, 103-105, 115, 120
caudal patch, 29, 94
collimator, 26
colour, 29, 39, 46, 54, 72, 73, 94, 108, 111
conception, 66-68, 119
Corbett, 47
Culicoides impunctatus, 12
deer farming, 8, 11, 35
deer forests, 6-8, 10-12, 40, 47, 58, 61, 62
defaecate, 74, 95
Denmark, 35, 74, 88, 99, 119, 120
diapause, 101, 119
dog, 107
Donald, 47
dragging, 17, 50, 53
droppings, 74
embryo sex, 60
epiphysis, 109

INDEX

eyes, 46, 47, 52, 93, 105
false rut, 86, 89, 111, 121
fat, 40, 60, 63, 69, 73, 77, 106
feeding, 38, 60, 71, 76, 91, 95, 96
foeti, 67, 68, 71, 96, 117, 119
foetus, 68
gestation, 35, 65, 66, 67, 119, 120
gralloch, 30, 50, 51, 52, 54, 56, 57, 95, 111, 112
grease, 12, 40
hair, 32, 39, 41, 53, 72, 73, 87, 93, 94, 97, 108, 117
hearing, 45, 105
Henry Evans, 39, 63, 64, 77, 81, 89
hoof clicking, 92
hummel, 35, 36, 37, 69
knife, 18, 50, 51, 108, 112
Lactation, 68, 69, 95, 115, 118
liver flukes, 52, 63, 122
lung worm, 63
melatonin, 39, 68, 93, 119
metabolic rate, 96
midges, 12, 41
milk hinds, 36, 60-62, 69, 71, 77, 89, 106, 115, 117
monocular, 18
monoestrous, 104
monoestry, 120
Munro, 47
paint and pins, 32, 108
parturition, 70, 118, 119
pedicle, 36, 76, 81, 88, 108
pelage, 41, 72, 93, 97, 117
pineal gland, 39, 68, 121
pregnancy, 92, 118, 120, 121
roaring, 36, 41, 42, 48, 49, 68
roe bag, 113
roe rings, 101, 102
ruminating, 71, 74, 91, 96, 97
rut, 11, 12, 37, 39-42, 48, 49, 60, 63, 67, 68, 71, 76, 85, 86, 89, 96, 101, 118, 121

scent, 45, 52, 70, 78, 85, 100, 105, 114
sounds, 73
telescope, 18
tempus pinguedinis, 40
territory, 85, 90, 98, 102, 115
testicles, 36, 39, 72, 99
testosterone, 12, 36, 39, 42, 49, 72, 85, 89, 98, 119
tooth sectioning, 77
tooth wear, 77, 80, 111
trajectory, 23
tusks, 55, 111
velvet, 12, 35-37, 39, 48, 68, 73, 78, 85, 87, 89, 90, 98, 119
venison, 12, 35, 40, 50, 60, 86
vision, 46
weights, 9, 12, 37, 56, 57, 84
yeld hinds, 60, 68, 77, 95